THE NOVELS OF C. P. SNOW

THE NOVELS OF
C. P. SNOW

A Critical Introduction

SUGUNA RAMANATHAN

© Suguna Ramanathan 1978

First published 1978 by
THE MACMILLAN PRESS LTD
London and Basingstoke
Associated companies in Delhi
Dublin Hong Kong Johannesburg Lagos
Melbourne New York Singapore Tokyo

Printed in Hong Kong

British Library Cataloguing in Publication Data

Ramanathan, Suguna.
  The Novels of C. P. Snow
  1. Snow, Charles Percy, *Baron Snow*—
  Criticism and interpretation
  I. Title
  823'.9'12   PR6037.N58Z/
  ISBN 0-333-23480-4

*To my husband Krishna and
my children Vaidehi and Vikram*

Contents

Preface

I started reading the novels of C. P. Snow over ten years ago, long before this book was ever thought of. With each volume that I read, Baudelaire's phrase 'mon semblable, mon frère' would pass through my mind, and when I noted that Snow, in his recent biography of Trollope, has quoted the first half of Baudelaire's line, 'Hypocrite lecteur', I was surprised and happy. It seemed like a sanction of some sort, a signal to set down something of my own response to Snow's novels. Several full studies on Snow have appeared before this one and I gratefully acknowledge the enlarging of my understanding that the work of Jerome Thale, Frederick Karl, R. G. Davis and R. Rabinovitz, in particular, has brought about. Many excellent articles which are listed in the bibliography also helped immensely.

The reason I felt that yet another study might be useful is that most of the books cited do not take Snow's later novels into account. The *Strangers and Brothers* sequence was completed only in 1970 and Snow has written two novels and a biography since then. The books mentioned above stop with *Corridors of Power*; Frederick Karl's fine study, *C. P. Snow: The Politics of Conscience*, stops with *The Affair*. The turn that Snow's work has taken since then, though illuminatingly touched on by Malcolm Bradbury in an essay, has not received much attention. It seemed to me, therefore, that a fresh assessment of Snow's significance as a novelist, surveying the whole body of his serious work, would not be wholly futile. I have included all his novels from *The Search* to *In Their Wisdom* in this study, omitting his two earliest works, *Death Under Sail* (a detective story) and *New Lives for Old* (a piece of science fiction), because they do not appear to be characteristic of his more serious preoccupations.

If Snow, as a novelist, is absorbed by the outer surface, he is equally so by an examination of the inner life; if the individual fascinates him, so do groups; if, at one level he is largely a meliorist, at another he is starkly gloomy. In this thesis I have considered his fourteen serious novels from different angles, and I trust that the stress of the individual chapters will underline the different aspects of Snow's fiction that can engage our interest.

Chapter 1, 'Sensibility and Form', attempts to define the unusual nature of Snow's imaginative impulse and the basic attitudes that underlie it. His need for a start in actual experience, often his own, and his problems with form are also discussed in some detail. Chapter 2, 'The Social Setting', discusses Snow's handling of the changing social scene in Britain over a span of fifty years. Chapter 3, 'The Examined Life', concerns itself with individuals, with their inner lives and their search for a meaningful moral code. Chapter 4, 'Groups and Enclaves' deals with Snow's understanding of men in conference. Chapter 5, 'The Darkening Vision', describes the gradual change in Snow's outlook from hopefulness to gloom and suggests possible reasons for this growing pessimism. Chapter 6 goes into the matter of Snow's technique – his success or otherwise in the delineation of his characters, and his deliberately cultivated plain style.

Snow has said in his preface to the three-volume edition of *Strangers and Brothers* that he has revised his earlier editions somewhat. During most of the time spent in the preparation of this book, however, the uniform three-volume edition was not available to me, and I was reluctant to forsake my old familiar friends, the Penguin editions, when it came to quotations from the text. In addition, I feel that the revisions have partially meant the sacrifice of Snow's original spontaneous growth as a writer. The growth of the writer from youth to age is reflected in the style itself; the later toning-down of the *The Light and the Dark*, for instance, is the work of an older man. It seemed to me that an aesthetic dimension was lost even while a homogeneous impression was gained; so I decided to use the earlier versions.

In the body of the text *The Times Literary Supplement* is referred to as *TLS* and the *Review of English Literature* as *REL*. In each chapter the first reference to a work is cited in full; references to the work thereafter are in a convenient abbreviated form.

C. P. Snow has aroused a fair amount of critical antipathy. I felt, in swimming sometimes against the tide, that if I could communicate something of the freedom from fanaticism so characteristic of this writer, and something also of his skill, it would be a task worth doing. Reading his novels has not only brought me hours of pleasure; it has made me understand better the contemporary notion of morality and given me the feel of contemporary social life.

The pleasantest part is this – recalling the many people who helped in the writing of this book. Lord Snow answered my many letters with patience and friendliness and showed me the greatest imaginable kindness and warmth when eventually we met. Professor K. R. Chandrashekaran, until recently University Professor of English, Gujarat University, provided useful criticism and restored my flagging confidence. Professors Calvin Bedient, John Espey and Richard Lehan, all of the English Department, University of California, Los Angeles, read different chapters and saved me from many lapses in logic and taste. My uncle, Professor S. V. Venkateswaran, Department of Atmospheric Sciences, University of California, Los Angeles, involved himself completely in my work, setting aside all other pressures and demands. His literary tact, scientific breadth and insistence on cogent argument have helped me more than I can say. Mr Paul Boytinck very kindly revised the bibliography for Snow's fiction and other selected writings. Meena Bhat and Sarvar Khambatta helped in the taking of notes and the compiling of the index. My father-in-law, Professor K. R. Ramanathan, was a constant source of encouragement and sympathy. The greatest debt is to my husband, Krishna Ramanathan, who revived my old academic ambitions and made many personal sacrifices to see this work completed. His generosity and unselfishness, from start to finish, have been unlimited.

To all of these people, my grateful thanks.

SUGUNA RAMANATHAN

July 1977

1 Sensibility and form

The reaction of C. P. Snow against modernism in general and the aesthetic novel in particular has become part of literary history. It is now pretty generally agreed that Snow is a contemporary[1] who regards himself as part of a continuing tradition, who unreservedly hailed the scientific and technological revolution, initially at any rate, and was preoccupied as much with the world of man's social, political and public interests as with the examination of his inner life. Such was the critics' assessment of Snow in the sixties and they were, of course, right in the main. But viewed today, in the shadowed light of the later novels, he appears as a writer who, besides carrying on within the old tradition of the realistic novel, was groping, fumbling towards the expression of a peculiar, individual, extra-literary sensibility.

Admittedly he has not altogether succeeded in finding a form which adequately connects outer and inner, and he is still better at some things than at others. Yet if there are scattered failures they are interesting ones, forcing us to pose anew the question of what constitutes art; whether the term can be stretched to include writing so steadfastly outside the aesthetic fold, and whether the brooding, dry, apparently simplistic, essentially rational ruminations are not a fresh, disguised aspect of the imagination itself.

No other writer of note, not even H. G. Wells, has stood so definitely outside the literary tradition. No other writer has so deliberately avoided metaphor, and few have displayed less animal vitality and high spirits than C. P. Snow. Yet the stamina, the staying-power, that has produced his fourteen serious novels strikes one as emanating from an unusual creative energy, from something more than a mere stubborn will to write. Whatever it is that informs the solid world of his fiction bears little resemblance to Coleridge's shaping, esemplastic power. It has generally been assumed, ever since Dryden, that it is not by the observation of life that art is formed but by the shaping of the raw material through an active power which affects the very act of perceiving. In Snow's novels art *is* formed through observation of the most ordinary kind. But the recapitulative sweep, the endless process of turning back and thinking over, gradually cocoons the ordinariness and changes it into someting slightly different, something dimly recognisable as an imaginative effect of the most unusual sort.

The reader is drawn into an activity which seems to be analytical and discursive but which eventually takes on an emotional colouring. This is difficult to illustrate, since the slow, cumulative process is itself the imaginative source; but one can try. Here is the last paragraph of *In Their Wisdom*:

> But there was another lesson a historian learned. They will also read our feelings and our experience quite differently from the way we lived them. The present couldn't imagine the ideas of the future, that is one of the certainties. It seemed equally certain, from what Ryle knew of history, that the future couldn't live again the existence of any present. For what it is worth, that is our own. We didn't know much, but that was something only we could know.
> A consolation? No, it just put us into perspective in the whole chain of lives, and that was humbling. Not that anyone should require humbling, Ryle thought, if he had lived in our time.[2]

Coming where those thoughts do, from the historian Ryle who has watched over the pursuits for money and love, has been torn by an old man's emotion and sensuality himself, has watched a friend die, voted England into the Common Market, seen another friend benefit from a risky brain operation, reflected on a variety of changes and events – coming from Ryle, these thoughts sound just right and final, phrased and placed with fine literary tact at the close.

Here is another passage, chosen at random from *The Sleep of Reason*. Eliot is thinking of his old friend George, who has run completely to seed:

> It was a sexual temperament which only a man in other respects ab normally controlled could have coped with. That he wasn't and – so it seemed – in his later life didn't want to be. In the past I had thought that, despite his gusto and capacity for joy, he too had known remorse and hadn't cared to look back at the sight of what he had once been. I had thought so during the time, long before ... when Olive and I were friendly, and she, who gave none of us the benefit of the doubt, jeered at me for giving it to George. I had believed she didn't understand faith or aspiration, that she looked at men as strange as George through the wrong end of the telescope. That was true: and yet her view of George wasn't all that wrong, and mine had turned out a sentimentality. Curiously enough, it would have seemed a sentimentality to

George himself. To borrow the phrase he had just employed, he had lived 'according to his nature'. For him, that was justification enough. He wasn't one who felt the obligation to re-shape his life. *Of course* he could look back at the sight of what he had once been. If I – because of comradeship or my own moral needs – wished to invest him with the signs of remorse, then that was my misfortune: even if, as I sat with him that afternoon, it meant the ripping away of – what? part of my youth, or experience, or hope.[3]

This long excerpt, notable incidentally for the nice accuracy with which it catches idiomatic language, takes us through a fairly complicated analysis of the George Passant – Lewis Eliot relationship. Eliot had always felt there was a 'higher' streak in George which makes him rue his wasted life. Has that been mere sentimental illusion on Eliot's part? Or nostalgia? Or is there something in it after all? After so many years of association can Eliot's perception be altogether discarded? The anwer is left in doubt. Does one merely view the truth through one's own 'moral needs'? On the other hand, if one does not give the benefit of the doubt, would not all things be reduced to their lowest denominator? Is George what Eliot thinks of him when he is with Eliot, and what Olive thinks of him when he is with Olive? Quite a few questions about character and the perception of it have been raised. But more important, such reflections take on a grave emotional aspect to which the reader, having lived with these people over several novels and been drawn into the net of their relationship, cannot help responding.

This sort of comment provides the chief interest of the novels. Plot is not very important to Snow and no writing could be less sensuous. But reflective analysis, wrapping the whole novel around like a cloak, becomes a subdued manifestation of the rationally tempered imagination. Snow's intuition burns like a steady flame and he uses it to set going a contemplative process that bodies out each book. Without it there would be only a series of episodes. *The Light and the Dark*, for instance, consists largely of Eliot's analysis of his friend Roy Calvert. There is nothing by way of developed action. The young man swings from gaiety to depression, upwards and then again to the depths, a pattern that repeats itself through the whole book; then he dies. But Eliot's loving observation of each of these moods, his obsessed affection for the unusual, the contrast he draws between such a one and his greyer, more ordinary self – these reflections give the book a strength not immediately discernible on a casual reading. It is not so much the story of what happened to Roy Calvert as an account of Roy Calvert as understood by his friend.

Snow's comment can at times be brief and surprisingly illuminating when re-read: for instance, at the end of *The Masters*, Jago, having lost the election, speaks to Eliot of the celebration they would have had if he had won. Eliot comments:

He spoke very simply and freshly as though he had put the suffering on one side and was able to rest. I was certain that he was still *hoping*. In his heart, this celebration was still going to take place. I knew well enough how slow the heart is to catch up with the brute facts. One looks forward to a joy: it is snatched away at the last minute: and, hours later, there are darts of illusory delight when one still feels that it is to come. Such moments cheat one and pass sickeningly away. So, a little later, the innocence ebbed from Jago's face. 'There will be no celebration for my friends', he said. 'I shall not even know how to meet them. I don't know who they are.'[4]

Reflections like these preside over every novel and no single passage can convey the overall impact. The build-up is muffled and gradual but the effect works itself out. The comments do not appear very striking at first; they do not feed the sensuous life; their tone seems dry. Yet imperceptibly they sink into the reader; their drab appearance is the secret of their power; seldom has the ordinary world been set down so completely in its ordinariness. We are used to seeing reality bathed anew, to being startled into an awareness of new relationships. Snow's fiction offers us none of this. Helen Gardner's complaint that Snow's evocation of Anglo-Jewish life is true but not revelatory, casts no new light,[5] goes to the heart of the matter; but precisely what she sees as a weakness I find rare and interesting. The absence of vision itself can appeal to the imagination in an odd way.

This is not to say that his collection of dry-as-dust details will by itself do; only those of his novels live for us in which there runs an emotional undercurrent threading the observations of his judgement. To read *The New Men*, for instance, is to be aware of a light withdrawn. The apparatus is all there: conferences, dilemmas, busy men and women, but vitality, subdued at the best of times, is missing. The distinction is a very fine one and the undercurrent something sensed, for *Corridors of Power*, equally dry and formally weak, has that vitality.

What of the world-view that shapes this sensibility? The world for Snow *is* governable; scientific advancement and man's intellect have made 'old Mother Nature' sit up and beg. If he uses his gifts of imagination and reason man can extract some sort of meaning and be fairly contented. Most of Snow's novels, right up till the last four, give us that sort of argument. In the latter novels, though technique remains as traditional as ever, there is a growing loss of assurance that the world can be manipulated or even that rational behaviour is its own reward. Still, on the whole it would be true to say that Snow is on the side of those who view life as understandable and meaningful. However difficult it is to arrive at an equilibrium, it *can* be reached.

Given this attitude, marriage, family, career and social responsibility all acquire importance. For the aesthetic writer the ordinary activities of life may be used to underline something much wider than themselves, to add up to some statement about human fate, but otherwise they seem irrelevant, futile, even slightly degrading, certainly never interesting for their own sake; whereas in a novel like *Corridors of Power* or *The Masters*, the way the votes fall is crucial in its own limited context; or human begins at a committee are described for themselves alone, because of the author's preoccupation with the variety of human nature, not for anything beyond that. Clearly then, the writer begins with the smaller pieces of the puzzle, closely observing them, gathering the bits empirically and fitting them together. Whether a fully composed picture will emerge he cannot say, but he is open and receptive to all possibilities.

Nothing could be further from the pattern-finding, highlighting, formalising approach to life of the aesthetic novelists. Snow distrusts their preoccupation with the individual sensibility (what he calls the 'personalist vision') and their worship of form and words. Angus Wilson, also a realistic writer, but much more sympathetic than Snow to the experimental school pinpoints social outsiderness as the main reason for the reaction against aesthetic novelists in England:

> No sharpness of visual image, no increased sensibility, no deeper penetration of the individual consciousness, whether by verbal experiment or Freudian analysis, could fully atone for the frivolity of ignoring man as a social being, for treating personal relationships and subjective sensation in a social void ... There is about Stephen Dedalus ... or Mrs. Ramsey ... a sort of intellectual and emotional separateness from responsible society at large which most people experience so fully as adolescents.[6]

Snow rejects the aesthetic novelists on moral and intellectual grounds also, maintaining that there has been an abdication of responsibility. Too much concern about the unique tragedy of the individual has meant an indifference to society's claims, a social callousness which is morally wrong. For Snow, loving one's neighbour is one way of inheriting eternal life. He never, of course, puts it in those terms, but the Christian ethic of concern for one's fellows (the brotherliness of his sequence) is very important to him. Religion seems to count for little with him; he is as secular a writer as possible; but the message at the bottom is the same. As a contrast, Joyce's *Portrait of the Artist as a Young Man* with its elaborate Roman Catholic background, has much less of that ethic than any of the books of this agnostic writer. Joyce presents the ritual of the church in great detail and consciously rejects its call. Snow apparently rejects the ritual and faith of Christian dogma, but he preaches its ethic all the same. Joyce's Stephen Dedalus is outside society, Snow's Lewis Eliot is well entrenched within it and alive to his responsibility as a member of it. That sort of aliveness would mean spiritual death to Stephen Dedalus for his desire to forge the conscience of his race wells up from entirely different springs. Meaningfulness in life is found in opposite directions by these two.

In rejecting the dominance of aesthetic over moral values Snow is, of course, in the tradition of George Eliot, scrutinising life from a moral point of view. Without sitting in judgement upon any human type, he is enquiring in the words of Jerome Thale, into 'the psychic price of success and fulfilment in a world like ours'. If men have to compromise, which are the areas? The only crime he considers unpardonable is hardness of heart; this is implied in the title given to the whole sequence *Strangers and Brothers*, a nice understated phrase stressing compassion that does not lapse into sentimentality. The struggles of conscience faced by modern men living within society and longing for its rewards are the moral issues that most concern Snow. One who keeps his integrity, condemns none and does his best for others, is his version of today's hero. Success should never be sought for its own sake, and, when it comes, should never disjoin remorse from power. Humanitarian concern is the dominant value in Snow's scheme. Second to that is the search of the individual for self-understanding and personal fulfilment. L. P. Hartley notes that in the rapidly changing society of today one of the great dangers is that the individual 'snowed under by the mass of suggestions, directions, orders and ready-made designs for living to which he is exposed, should be submerged and lost in the community'.[7] The romantic aesthetes' reply to this would be to stand outside the social pale and scorn its rewards. A modern writer like Beckett does not even cherish the supremacy of art. *Nothing matters.* But to Snow life does matter and to live it as fully and as generously as one can is an endeavour worth trying.

If Snow rejects the world view of the modernist writers he rejects their experimentation with techniques no less. This ground has been so fully covered by critics that all that is needed here is to note what Snow has said in a fairly recent article on Trollope about the verbal rendering of thought processes. He says it is not always a stream and only partly conscious; it is not always or often verbal, and not much of this is worth communicating in words. He declares outright that the verbalised presentation does not satisfy him; his own thought-process seems to him different:

> Mine doesn't happen very much in that fashion, certainly not often and not as a continuous process; it is usually less discrete, less momentary, less verbal, and less immediately expressible in verbal terms. It contains far greater elements of unverbalized elements.[8]

Snow's recognition that thought for him is not immediately expressible in verbal terms explains his antipathy to the poetic novelists. To the poetic imagination and, at a remove, to the trained literary sensibility, words, the right words in the right order, come instinctively, as leaves to the tree. Snow has, it is true, forged over the years a distinctive style for himself, but he seems not to be one for whom words arrange themselves immediately. Consequently, he distrusts this facility; his imagination is not essentially a poetic one. Rhythms do not pulsate obviously in his prose; it is a ruminating quality that gives it its own kind of distinction. Uneasy with symbols, he confesses that in reading E. M. Forster and L. P. Hartley, two modern novelists who underline their symbolism, 'one is, or at least, I am more comfortable elsewhere in their work'.[9]

Such then is the sensibility of this highly intelligent and interesting novelist. Judged by any aesthetic yardstick it may seem simplistic, naïve, unappreciative of the beauty and complexity of vision and too rooted in the everyday scene.

Snow's realism itself is closer to actual fact, less transmuted and more faithful to his own experiences than one might expect from a writer of fiction. The sequence was to reflect the lifetime experiences of the author and the changing quality of social life; it is for this reason that Snow has deliberately given the series an open-endedness and a receptivity to changes both in society and within Lewis Eliot himself as he passes from youth to age. The *TLS* in a leading article called 'Experience of a Lifetime' discusses the different novel sequences of Snow, Doris Lessing, Anthony Powell and Lawrence Durrell. It observes that the common characteristic of these sequences is that they attempt the fictionalisation of the personal experiences of the novelists, and that the novelists themselves are present within their novels. It quotes Stephen Dedalus's remark that the artist, like God, may remain outside his creation, invisible, refined out of existence, indifferent, paring his finger nails! Such a stand, the article concludes, would seem absurd to the contemporary writers mentioned.[10]

Interesting questions arise: how much of the novelist's autobiographical material is to be translated wholesale into fiction? How much of it is to be worked upon by the imagination? How literal can realism get?

In Snow's novels there are certainly elements which are very largely autobiographical. They reflect the deepest experiences as well as a large number of superficial and external details from his life, and yet maintain a fictional veneer. In the last two novels of the *Strangers and Brothers* sequence, Snow has troubled very little to retain the fictional disguise. He has said in an interview that Lewis Eliot is largely himself:

> I would have thought that in depth Lewis Eliot is myself. In a good many of his situations and in a good many of his external appearances he is not me, but in any serious and interesting sense, he is.[11]

Rabinovitz has convincingly demonstrated how much similarity there is between Snow and his protagonists Lewis Eliot and Arthur Miles. They all come from poor families, have ambitious mothers, dislike music, like cricket, and are interested in the administrative side of their profession. Both Snow and Eliot keep notebooks in which they keep jottings, and both become writers at about the same time in their lives. Arthur Miles leaves science because of an oversight in a piece of his research, as apparently Snow did.[12]

One can go much further in tracing similarities in the light of the later novels and Lady Snow's memoirs. The fathers of both Lewis Eliot and Snow lived to a great age and died in their eighties; both were secretaries of local choirs or music associations; and both appear to have been mild but quiet and independent, refusing to live with their sons. Lewis Eliot throughout the series is depicted as tone-deaf. In *The Affair* Lewis Eliot remarks that he is completely left out while the others enjoy Berlioz.[13] In *Corridors of Power* Eliot is surprised to see Hector Rose at a concert knowing he is tone-deaf, and adds that he (Eliot) did not care for music himself and had only gone to please Margaret.[14] Lady Snow describes in her book of memoirs that her husband likes to describe himself as tone-deaf.[15] Though they are not musical, both Snow and Eliot are appreciative of pictures. There are many illusions to Sisleys, water-colour collections, Piranesi prints, and Sidney Nolans. From Lady Snow's book we learn about the Snows' private collection of pictures, especially their prized Sidney Nolan, the original Kelly.[16]

In *The Sleep of Reason* and *Last Things* the fictional disguises have worn very thin. The eye-operation in *The Sleep of Reason* is autobiography down to the detal of Eliot attending a University meeting with an eye-patch over the detached retina.[17] In this book, first published in 1968, Eliot mentions how he has been charged in public with plagiarism and how painful it has been to be the focus of an attack on that account. This seems to me to be a reference to F. R. Leavis's notorious attack on Snow in the early sixties and the controversy that raged thereafter about the 'Two Cultures'. The charges were of course different but the experience of being attacked is drawn from Snow's own life. The second eye-operation described in *Last Things*, in which Eliot has a cardiac arrest for nearly four minutes, is plain autobiography, as is evident from Lady Snow's memoirs. Young Charles Eliot, the son of Lewis and Margaret Eliot, is apparently drawn after Philip, Snow's son. Like his original, Charles Eliot goes to Eton on a scholarship, has a brilliant academic record there, spends a year travelling all over the East when he is sixteen and likes the writings of J. R. Tolkien. Even the housekeepers for Eliot and Snow are both of Latin origin (Italian for Eliot, Spanish for Snow).[18]

Austin Davidson, art critic and father-in-law of Lewis Eliot, is based on G. H. Hardy, the famous Cambridge mathematician and Snow's close friend. The details that appear in the portrait of Hardy in Snow's biographical sketches *Variety of Men* correspond closely with those about Austin Davidson in the sequence. The association with Bloomsbury, the bright brown eyes, the dislike of opening preambles in conversation, the faith in examinations – all these are exactly the same for both. When Hardy first met Snow he put him through a considerably stiff 'viva' on cricket. When Davidson meets Eliot for the second time he puts him through a 'brisk viva' on his knowledge of pictures.[19] Both Hardy and Davidson dislike mechanical contrivances like the telephone and both say: 'If you *fancy* yourself at the telephone, there is one under the stairs [or in the next room].'[20] Both have a passion for games of their own invention played with teams. Hardy was passionately interested in the cricket scores; Davidson in the Stock Exchange quotations. Even that last modification seems to derive from a remark Maynard Keynes, the well-known economist, once made to Hardy that if he had read the Stock Exchange quotations half an hour daily with the same concentration he gave the cricket scores, he could not have helped becoming a rich man.[21] Both Hardy and Davidson had coronary thrombosis and sank into apathy thereafter. Both attempted suicide, took too many pills, vomited, fell and hit their heads on the lavatory basin, and had black eyes the next morning. When Eliot visits Davidson in hospital the morning after, Davidson mocks himself for having made a mess of the suicide attempt, and Eliot has to respond in a similar sarcastic fashion, saying many people, notably the German officers Beck and Stulpnagel, failed to make a go of it. This account corresponds exactly with Snow's account of his own conversation with Hardy, the morning after *his* suicide attempt. The same German generals are mentioned in the same ironic tone. Both Hardy and Davidson studied the swelling of their ankles and were pleased when they found their oedema to be a shade less. Snow has said in his preface to *Variety of Men* that the conversations recorded are drawn from his memory which is generally good. He also says that of all the nine people of whom he has written biographical sketches only G. H. Hardy has been used as a character in his fiction but 'in a form so transmogrified that no one has ever noticed'. To anyone who has closely read both the novels and *Variety of Men*, the resemblance is inescapable.

Real life and personal experience obviously provide Snow with some of his material. In a recent biography of Trollope, so sympathetically written that one feels he is really also talking about himself,[22] he mentions Trollope's need to start with the real, the actual, before his imagination could get to work. He needed a hint or a start. Snow observes:

No novelist – no good novelist that is – can produce his people out of a complete vacuum.[23]

It is clear from all this that Snow has a much more *literal* imagination than many writers. His sharp observation of people and scenes and his accurate memory help him to transfer chunks of experience untouched into fiction.

Such evidence may well be used by his critics to underline his simplified approach to art and the poverty of his creative resources; that is the obvious criticism. More interesting perhaps is the recognition that documentary recall of fact after years of pondering can be used imaginatively and effectively.

There remains the vexed question of his attitude to form. From the first Snow rejected the Coleridgean notion of organic form and reacted sharply against the literariness of literature. He admits to Frank Kermode in an interview that for him there is no separate world of art, no shaping impulse from within imposing a pattern on the flux of events, no discontinuity between the real world and the world of art. It follows that the 'delighted manipulation of elements that already exist in an autonomous world of art' is an activity that Snow does not regard as valid, for himself at any rate. When asked by Frank Kermode whether his being a scientist had conditioned the view of reality presented in his books, Snow replies:

Quite a bit ... certainly part of my training would make me suspicious of a lot of the categories which certain writers think in, and also would give me, I think, a rather simpler view of the kind of truth I should like to aim at.[24]

Consistent with his 'rather simpler view of truth', Snow sets out to write the complete realistic novel in which society and the individual are properly placed without either of them usurping the dominant role. He himself describes his novels as attempting a resonance between man and society. This resonance is achieved as a slow, gathering effect in a sequence of eleven novels, *Strangers and Brothers*. It appears to me that the range and breadth of the sequence attain a total significance which a single novel within it does not alway seem to possess.

However, Raymond Williams complains that for want of a firm grip on form Snow has failed in his attempt to write the complete realistic novel. To throw in a little bit of the sex-life of a scientist in the middle of numerous scientific conferences, as Snow does in *The New Men*, cannot make, he says, the personal and social combine in a meaningful way.[25] Many other critics have felt that Snow has underrated form more than any important English novelist alive. In the interview with Frank Kermode mentioned earlier, where the novelists are classed into 'crystalline' and journalistic groups[26] Snow is quite happy to be placed in the second group and declares himself suspicious of myth. He does not mind, he says, 'formal patterning', but even this he does not regard as absolutely essential. This attitude on Snow's part is summarised by Bernard Bergonzi:

Indeed the whole burden of Snow's attitude to his craft suggests that too much concern with language and construction is actively undesirable, since it may lead the novelist away from the everyday intercourse of decent rational men into a realm of unhealthy aestheticism.[27]

But Pamela Hansford Johnson reminds us that it is silly to imagine that a novelist of his standing has given little or no thought to problems of aesthetics and form and appears to welcome a more casual approach to form:

> Writers of moral and social vision simply cannot work within the confines of an obtrusively lyrical art-form. He cannot work for the sake of form; he has to make the form worth for him. The passion of form for form's sake very nearly ran the English novel into complete sterility.[28]

Even if one accepts that Snow is not totally unconscious of form, one is still hard put to say that a consistent degree of form is maintained in all his novels. Some of the novels are formally better than others and some verge on formlessness. Good from the point of view of form are *The Masters* (written fairly early) and *In Their Wisdom* (his latest novel). In *The Masters* unity is imposed by space, time and action. The entire action takes place within the confines of a college during the period when the Master of the college is dying of cancer; the plot itself revolves around the outcome of an election for a new Master. With the plot thus taking care of itself, Snow's analysis and ruminations about human nature in the novel fall in place. *In Their Wisdom* likewise has a strong suspense element: will Jenny Rastall win the appeal against her father's will? With that unifying, suspenseful question at the core, Snow is able freely to shift his scenes and introduce as many characters as his interest in the variety of men leads him to do without seriously impairing the sense of form.

Because Snow's main preoccupations are seldom concerned with form, without an underpinning plot, his novels tend to lose shape altogether. This is because the chief formal devices of the writer – myth and symbol – are deliberately rejected by him, with the result that if the plot itself does not provide the shape, his novels quite frequently take on an amorphous diffusiveness. For example, a novel like *The Sleep of Reason* falls well on the side of the journalistic division. Snow has made some concession to 'formal patterning' by framing the novel with old Mr Eliot alive at the beginning and dead at the end, but this by itself is not enough. The novel lacks a centre and falls into two parts: Lewis Eliot's involvement with dismissed university students, and the trial of two girls for murder. Eliot's eye-operations are in no way relevant to either issue and, absorbing as the accounts of them are, contribute largely to the overall shapelessness. Snow had originally planned to write a novel called *The Devoted* dealing with a crucial event in Eliot's life. In a personal communication to me he admits to having cannibalised it, using parts of it in *The Sleep of Reason*, which is based very largely on the Moors Murders of 1965. This may partially explain the formal slackness of this novel. A re-reading might indeed reveal that the unrestrained sexual libertinism of the dismissed students is not unrelated to the sensational torturing and murder of the child by Kitty Pateman and Cora Ross, the lesbian pair. Too much permissiveness, the sexually violent undertow, the breakdown of tradition – these are presumably part of the pattern, but that pattern does not emerge inevitably from the novel and has to be read into it.

Corridors of Power, again an impressive novel on many counts and an important summary of the political climate of a decade, shares this uncertainty about form. The bits about Roger Quaife's extra-marital relationship with Ellen Smith do not fit into the rest of what is mainly a political and social novel. It looks for a while as if it will be one of the springs of action determining Quaife's future, but it fizzles out irrelevantly. Was it put in to make the hero more of an individual? If so, it comes in at random, superficially; it does not arise from a strongly grasped apprehension of Quaife as a person in a particular society. Clearly, Snow's attention in this novel is directed towards the political issue. He has thrown in the Ellen Smith theme apparently without sufficiently working out its place in the scheme of the novel.

Snow then does not believe in organic form, or, to use Iris Murdoch's words, a 'crystalline, closely-coiled' structure. He is comfortable only with a freer and looser method in which he can discuss a number of different things without having to weave them into a highly unified whole.

It would, however, be a mistake to think that he is wholly artless and naïve about structure. Because he is interested in re-creating the ordinariness of life, he deliberately avoids too much neatness of pattern, suggesting through looser form something of life's inherent untidiness. This is not to make the mistake of thinking that by being incoherent one evokes the impression of incoherence, or that by being boring oneself one can create boring characters who are delightful to read about. To suggest incoherence or dullness requires by itself some sort of design on the part of the author. So much of design at least Snow has in mind, but he avoids strong formalism so as to establish the impression of contingency, of events happening at random. In many of his novels what there is of form arises out of concepts of character as they make or mar their lives.

The *roman-fleuve* structure imposes a unity of sorts on Snow's novel sequence. The reappearance of characters and their growth, ageing and deaths with the progression of the sequence serve as binding elements on the plethora of events surrounding them. The ravages of time on people whom we first encountered as young and hopeful men tend to give the series a distancing effect. It might be argued that the unity thus provided is external and superficial. So it might seem for the space of a novel or two; but cumulatively the novels within the series draw together and form a whole.

Recurring preoccupations also draw the different novels together: possessive love, the pursuit of power, the need to find an emotional and moral balance. Lewis Eliot's mother had made too many demands on him; his friend Charles March breaks away from such obsessive parental affection. Eliot's son, young Charles Eliot, also leaves home and strikes out on his own, but now there is no final break as there had been in the case of Charles March with *his* father. Eliot has learned enough about possessiveness (both from direct experience of his mother's affection and observed experience of his friend) to school it and give his son his freedom. Also, this is a different generation; parental authority has become something of an anachronism. Young Charles moves quietly into his mistress's house, expecting no fuss from his parents. Nor do they create a scene beyond a certain recorded exchange of dismayed glances. Again, when Lewis Eliot in *Last Things* turns down an offer to join the government, it takes us back to his ambitions as a young man in *Time of Hope* when he had risked all he had on his will to succeed. With the passage of time, Eliot's preoccupation with power is gradually blunted and mellowed. Thus, through recurring themes, Snow holds his many novels together.

The most important unifying factor of the sequence is simply the protagonist Lewis Eliot himself. It is his way of thinking and feeling that we grow familiar with; through his eyes we watch people and events unfolding. By the end of the series we know his measured tone as well as we know our own, merely because we have heard it so long. The novel in the sequence into which he enters least, *The Conscience of the Rich*, seems a sort of outsider in the family, perhaps because Charles March lives as a character more independently than Roy Calvert and George Passant. There is less of Lewis Eliot's filtering sensibility here, fewer exchanges between him and Charles, fewer observations and analyses, and more 'head-on' presentation of characters. Many critics have regarded it as the best in the series. Personally, I cannot find it as satisfying as some of the others in the sequence. The sort of effectiveness found in that novel has been achieved before, and in some cases better, by other novelists. What is uniquely interesting to me about the *Strangers and Brothers* series is Snow-Eliot's presence there, for one agrees with the *TLS* that 'in the last analysis the quality of the novelist's mind is everything'.[29] For novels outside the sequence that particular tone or attitude is not expected. As noted earlier, *In Their Wisdom* carries its own unity made up of a strong suspense element and a brooding sensitiveness not usually found together. Within the sequence, however, Lewis Eliot's presence is essential.

One point that has been repeatedly raised in discussing the unity and structure of Snow's novel sequence is the compartmentalisation of Lewis

Eliot's life. For instance, when Eliot is watching his friend Charles March through his struggles in *The Conscience of the Rich*, he is himself involved, as we know from an earlier novel *Time of Hope*, in courting Sheila Knight. But we never hear a word about it in that novel itself. Another example: when he tells us the story of Roy Calvert in *The Light and the Dark,* Eliot is himself going through misery in marriage which ends in his wife's suicide. But this never enters; it is kept for another novel, *Homecomings.* Critics have argued that this kind of rigid separation of his experiences points to a failure on Snow's part to integrate Eliot's varied experiences into a meaningful whole. Richard Lehan says, for example:

> He lacks Proust's and Faulkner's ability to convey simultaneity of action. The eight novels in Snow's sequence often present Lewis Eliot at the same moment in time, yet Eliot is always single-mindedly preoccupied.[30]

William F. Hall points to two possible reasons for this compartmentalisation of experience: either Snow is unable to integrate the various experiences of Eliot into a total unity, or Snow intends to convey that the ideal balance in his total experience is not achieved by Lewis Eliot an explanation favoured by Hall.[31]

Rubin Rabinovitz feels that by separating experiences Snow has missed a chance to employ fully the technique of resonance between what Eliot says and what he feels, the resonance which Snow had intended to be the inner design of his series.[32]

Bernard Bergonzi says that, for Eliot to emerge as a whole man, the different strands of his experience must be shown to intertwine and modify one another instead of being kept rigidly apart. He notes that Snow is like the Wilcoxes in Forster's *Howards End*, who did not handle human affairs in the bulk, but disposed of them 'item by item, sharply'.[33] Derek Stanford alone defends Snow's method as representative of life's laborious unwindings.[34]

It seems to me that Snow's method of compartmentalisation does not preclude the overall perspective which is provided by the cumulative technique itself. The last book in the sequence, *Last Things,* provides that perspective by looking back, drawing conclusions, making endings, yet closing on a note of continuation as young Charles Eliot goes off to the Middle East on his own. Here we find George Passant, hero of the earliest novel, dying alone in Belgium, broken and desolated, his fight for freedom having taken him through nightmare and ending in squalor; Francis Getliffe, who appears on the fringe of many of the earlier novels, dies of cancer, his scientific gift alive in his son; Roy Calvert is dead, but his daughter is here, with a child, a discarded husband, and a young lover. There is a roll-call of the dead sounding in Eliot's mind as he attends the memorial service of his old friend Getliffe, a very fitting obituary note. As for Eliot himself, the two main themes in his life – the pursuit of success in society and the individual's struggle to find personal happiness – are both played out here, and both recede and fade. His detachment from power and success is seen in his refusal to serve again in high office. His social role is over; he has been, long enough, a responsible citizen and a loyal friend. As an individual he faces the worst struggle, a terrible loneliness in the face of death. Even Margaret's voice is very far away, and his marriage, that centre of calm from which Eliot worked outward, is no longer of much use in this final trial. Yet nothing, not even that, is quite final. Eliot survives the cardiac arrest, goes back to the family circle and is once again involved, but now with a newly-gained sense of detachment. The book ends on that lifelike note – things go on, nothing stops, the heavens never fall, even the curtain doesn't finally come down.

This final volume provides the necessary perspective and resonance for the whole sequence. Though by itself it may seem to lack impact, as a comment on the rest it is highly significant.

The other novels are separate entities but as a series they still retain the *roman-fleuve* character with the result that the modifying effects of events and experience can be traced across them clearly – Eliot understanding his own nature; Eliot saddened by his friend's lot; Eliot sobered by life.

There are times when Snow's analytical preoccupation runs him into some trouble with his point of view. Lewis Eliot, who is himself a participant in the story, could not credibly be expected to gauge the mental processes of other characters in such intimate detail as he is in fact made out to do. This, it seems to me, raises a more basic difficulty than the coincidences of Eliot's just happening to be present at all the crises in the novels, which Bergonzi finds unrealistic.[35] This fact of Eliot's convenient presence on such occasions does not by itself seem to me to strain credibility much. Almost always, Eliot is connected through his job or his friendships with the crises. But the confidence with which he comments occasionally on what he could not possibly know makes one feel that the point of view, in spite of the first-person narration, is really that of the Omniscient Observer.[36] As an illustration, here is a passage from *The Light and the Dark* about Joan Royce falling in love with Roy Calvert:

> She found incredulously that he liked her. She heard him make playful love to her, and she repeated the words, like a charm, before she went to bed at night.[37]

Snow here wants us to understand something of Joan's lack of confidence in herself and yearning for Roy. But even as a sympathetic friend, Eliot could not have really known what Joan did, though he might have guessed intelligently at what she felt.

When Snow finally throws off the first-person narrative in his latest novel *In Their Wisdom*, he frees himself of what has at times acted as a restriction on his need to comment on his characters.

At the same time, Lewis Eliot in the *Strangers and Brothers* sequence is Snow's presence there, a persona for the novelist's mind. Gradually we grow very familiar with the quality of that mind: rational, ambitious, driven both to success and destruction, above all sympathetic and reluctant to condemn. It is with regret that we hear it for the last time in the closing volume, *Last Things*. Snow has remarked that while it was a relief to have completed the task he had set himself, he could not help a feeling of homesickness for the sequence which had taken up most of his life as a writer.[38]

There is not much, then, to be said in defence of the formal weakness of some of the novels. Snow has not evolved any special techniques to communicate his insights. Even when writing *Corridors of Power*, which he acknowledges as being an unusually complicated political novel involving a multitude of issues and people, he sticks to his conventional 'then this is what happened' approach. But the nature of his fascinating, separated and circumscribed insights is such that, at his best, the chronological sequential method of narration works well. To use Virginia Woolf's famous distinction, life for Snow is no luminous semi-transparent envelope but rather a series of gig-lamps symmetrically arranged. And why not? That is surely one valid way of regarding life. And this does not mean that Snow is unresponsive to the subtlety and complexity of human nature. He *is* responsive but he tackles each strand separately. The result is an impression of life filtered through the reasoning, ordering intellect – Lewis Eliot's perception of reality is what we get, one thing at a time.

If judgement seems to play too strong a part and imagination not enough one can only say that this impression may be true of any single novel, but that the scope of the entire enterprise and its power to make us look back and feel in touch with a whole age affect more than just the mind. Emotion stirs, perhaps uneasily, but the more touchingly for that very reason. Though he does indeed suggest that things are mostly what they seem, brings no awareness of the transcendent, gives little of what creative literature has taught us to expect, he demonstrates how, out of a thousand little bits and pieces, imagination can rise, wraith-like, and cast its Proustian light.

To sum up: Snow started out in deliberate reaction against the aesthetic novel, rejecting its basic response to life as much as its techniques. He prepared the way for the re-emergence of the realistic novel in which society and the individual interact in a symbiotic way. He raised concerns about the moral life one can lead in today's society. He explicitly rejected formalism; he was happier setting things down as seen and experienced. In some cases this amounted to recording experience 'in the raw' so to speak, unacted upon by any transforming power. He attempted to replace the myth-forming, symbol-making imagination by the reflective and ruminating intelligence which broods over his novels and lends them significance through comment and insight.

Snow is a writer who has to be read with patience – not, obviously, because of complex thought or style, but because of the gradual nature of his unfolding. For the casual hurried reader he offers little, neither exotic scene nor heightened style nor truth revealed in a lightning flash. To the committed addict he gives many rewards: the feel of half a century, and analysis and insight into human character so close to the bone that it comes almost as 'a muted shock'. We see again the ordinary world with 'utter familiarity and utter surprise'.

2 The social setting

Whatever reservations one may have for Snow's handling of the inner life, few can deny that he is one of the relevant commentators on the contemporary social scene. Outside the novels he has lectured on important public affairs and social issues, and within his fiction he has caught the changing tenor of half a century in Britain with a niceness and accuracy which must compel admiration from the most grudging critic. Even the *London Magazine*, which has consistently questioned Snow's stature as an artist, admits that the mirroring of the social scene is something which he does with competence.

Snow, who once remarked that the novel only breathes freely when it has its roots in society, has campaigned for years against the inward eye of the aesthetic novel. He believes that 'the moment you abstract man from society you don't make him more interesting, you don't make him deeper, you make him in the long run trivial'.[1] For him the highest sort of art is simply the rounded knowledge of human beings, a knowledge that comes from seeing men at work in society, living out their daily lives and reacting to the pressures and crises of the external world. Snow recognises that 'a novel is never really social history in the exact sense', but his *Strangers and Brothers* sequence has a structure which is clearly adapted to reflect the influence on the individual of society in flux.

The career of Lewis Eliot from poverty in a provincial town upwards to the most powerful offices in Whitehall reflects a changed society in which, though class and privilege still count, those gifted with wit and intellect are not barred from high positions. Eliot is not the only one who works his way up. In *Homecomings* there is a bright young official in the Treasury office called Douglas Osbaldistone. He comes from the real working class (Eliot from the fringe between the lower middle and the working), but is expected to rise higher in the Civil Service than even Sir Hector Rose, the son of an archdeacon with Oxford behind him. Social mobility, a marked twentieth-century characteristic in Britain, is suggested through characters of this sort. With enough ambition and will one can climb as high as one wants (or almost) in a meritocratic society. Walter Luke, the son of a dockyard hand, finishes up in the series as Lord Luke of Salcombe.

Class-consciousness, stronger in Britain than anywhere else, and changes in class structure are issues to which Snow is sensitive and alive. He illustrates two contrasting features of class in Britain. First, the old rigidity has certainly become more flexible; a poor boy from the Midlands can through education find his way into exclusive country houses. Second, in spite of the levelling influence of education, the old institutions of privilege and class snobbery stubbornly survive beneath the surface. Accents, titles, schools, universities – these continue to count, although the lack of them is not so much of a handicap as it used to be.

Snow merely records gradations of snobbery; he neither approves nor disapproves. In the early novels, the Boscastles are the real aristocrats with titles going back to the sixteenth century. Lady Muriel, Lord Boscastle's sister, has married a little beneath her, the master of a Cambridge college, plain Mr Vernon Royce. Lady Boscastle, so aristocratic, urbane and civilised, comes, Eliot discovers, from somewhere lower – the professional middle class. Eliot notes with surprise how much social distinctions matter to them:

> I had expected them to be less interested in social niceties than the middle classes were. I had not found it so. Nothing could be further from the truth. They did it on a grander scale, that was all.[2]

Among the Fellows of the college Winslow is definitely gentry (though without a title), drawn from the country squirearchy, the only one whom Lady Muriel considers an equal, and so sure of his class that he can afford to say that he is the son of a draper. Everyone knows that the draper was unmistakably 'county'. At the other end of the scale is Walter Luke from Plymouth dockyard, with brash splutteringness to match, none of your polite veneer, yet open to life as many of the stuffed shirts are not. Roy Calvert, the brilliant scholar, is the son of a rich provincial tradesman, but has so much innate style and *élan* that he has an unquestioned entrée into high society. He is always Roy to Lady Muriel, whereas Lewis Eliot, lacking such elegance, remains to the end 'Mr – er – Eliot'.

English society, as seen by Snow, is neither class-ridden nor entirely privilege-free. When it is brought to the notice of Azik Schiff, a very rich Jewish financier, that his step-daughter is going around with Pat, Martin Eliot's son, he tells Lewis Eliot that he knows that the Eliots are a good family though he is clearly aware of their lowly origins. This makes Eliot comment on the doors that can be thrown open by education and training:

He knew precisely where we came from. But he meant something different. Azik saw, much more clearly than most Englishmen, what English society had become. It was tangled, it was shifting its articulations, but in it men like Martin had their place.[3]

In spite of the loosening of the class structure with the progress of the century, Eliot correctly perceives that there are segments of society which, at the core, have in fact hardened and become *more* rather than *less* rigid since his youth:

Its forms were crystallizing under our eyes into an elaborate and codified Byzantism, decent enough ... but not blown through by the winds of scepticism, or individual protest or sense of outrage which were our native air.[4]

Snow through Eliot observes that while education undoubtedly swells the ranks of the old élites, the old aristocrats have become more self-conscious, and as 'they lose their power and turn into ornaments, shut themselves up and exaggerate their distinguishing marks'.[5] With the gradual withdrawal of privilege which, according to Crawford in *The Affair*, gives one the direction of time's arrow, many of the aristocrats draw in their horns and defiantly conform to the old-established patterns – Eton and the Universities. There is a nice little sketch in *The Affair* of tea at the Skeffingtons where everyone plays a 'specifically English kind of Happy Families' by claiming friends highly placed or highly born:

County names, titled names, token names, they all chanted them as though the charmed circle were tiny and as though one kept within it by chanting in unison.[6]

There is also a picture of the lion-hunting Drawbells in *The New Men*, Mr Drawbell panting for his K.C. and Mrs Drawbell all too eager to have a real aristocrat in her drawing-room.

On the whole, however, Snow does not satirise the snobs; he merely records their existence. In fact, Kathleen Nott feels that he should have been more satiric. Picking out an account in *The New Men* where Eliot, dining with his Minister at an exclusive club, thinks of how pleased his poor, snobbish mother would have been to see him there, she comments tartly that Snow or Eliot seems 'as pleased as Mum herself'.[7]

Snow also exhibits examples of inverse snobbery – upper-class people assuming working-class mannerisms and speech. One such example is to be found in *The Affair* in the person of Lester Ince, who, Eliot decides, is a social fraud in reverse. Instead of climbing the social ladder, he wants to come down it, and Eliot remarks:

He was actually a doctor's son, born in the heart of the middle classes, educated like the quintessence of the professional bourgeoisie, middling prep school, middling public school. He insisted on behaving, talking and often feeling, as though he had come up from the ranks. Just as with the other kind of social mimic, one listened to his speech. Beneath the curious mixture of what he thought, often not quite accurately, to be lower-class English or happy-go-lucky American, one could hear the background of an accent as impeccably professional as Arthur Brown's.[8]

In this case, Ince is not expressing any protest but savouring the greater freedom which he imagines comes from identifying with the working class. Here is an implicit recognition that class, cultivation, polite behaviour or whatever, do not always work to one's advantage but may at times hamper freedom and impose too many inhibiting restrictions.

Accent, the way one speaks, as every reader of *Pygmalion* knows, is so important for social acceptance in England that the aspiring unconsciously shed their provincialisms and take on the protective colouring of standard English. In Snow's novels there are numerous speculations on what accents reveal or betray. Sir Hector Rose (of gentle birth) marries again, and when Eliot meets his new wife he unerringly picks out her lower-middle-class origin:

> ... she didn't belong to any sort of professional world, she came perhaps – there was a residual accent – from origins like mine.[9]

Eliot mentions in some of the novels that to anyone without an English ear these facts would not be so obvious or important.[10] He himself, perhaps because he has risen from the lower levels, is acutely aware of inflection and intonation. Eliot, of course, is reflecting his creator's sensitiveness to speech, for in novels outside the *Strangers and Brothers* sequence, where there is no Eliot, there are comments of a similar nature. *In Their Wisdom*, for instance, has a scene in which Jenny Rastall, the poorish middle-aged daughter of a rich man recently dead, and Reginald Swaffield, a self-made, bumptious and flauntingly wealthy industrialist, are talking. Snow muses thus on the scene:

> If James Ryle, who had travelled up through layers of society, had been listening to them, he would have known that her voice was still undiluted upper middle-class, clear, unsloppy, not attacking but not a mumble, perceptibly louder than those of the contemporary young. While she, who had travelled down through similar layers, was puzzling about Swaffield's accent. She couldn't place it. Actually, the base was midland but overlaid by a veneer of Illinois American. . . . Before the war, he had tried to make a living there.[11]

What do all these keen remarks add up to? Do they have any value at all in the novel? I believe they do. They point to a dispassionate curiosity about people in society and an aliveness to nuance, in themselves of immense value to the novelist. The other value is the obvious one. These observations add an extra dimension to his description of the quality of social life in his time.

Snow himself remains fascinated but aloof. He seems to agree that there are inbred differences that class is responsible for. Eliot feels that his wife Margaret and her father Austin Davidson have a kinship of the nerves from which he himself is excluded.[12] But Snow does not sentimentalise the upper classes as Galsworthy did. One recalls the quivering refinement of Dinny Charwell ('A Botticelli angel') and her oh-so-poetic lover Wilfred Desert, son of Lord Mullyon, in *End of the Chapter* and one feels that Galsworthy had romanticised them and seen them through a glamorous haze. Snow escapes that trap. His aristocrats, Lord Boscastle and Lord Hillmorton, to name two, are every whit as petty, anxious and narrow as the Patemans of Passants. People do not get prettified the higher up you go. Snow himself is as interested in mild old Mr Eliot as in the influential and powerful people in the House of Lords.

Another aspect of the social scene recorded by Snow is the emergence of the scientists as a social force, in the depiction of whom Snow unerringly strikes original and authentic notes. The part played by scientists as advisers to government is clearly reflected in *Corridors of Power* and *The New Men*. Snow has seen how the wheels go round. He was in Cambridge during England's most exciting scientific period and he has been a Minister in the Cabinet. His ability to convert all that experience into good fiction gives him a unique standing among novelists. His experience in science and politics is cleverly carried over into his presentations of the politician in his chamber and of the scientist in and out of his laboratory.

I shall now examine in greater detail how Snow has recorded in his individual novels the dominant social mood of different phases of the last fifty years.

The first published novel of the sequence *Strangers and Brothers* was itself called *Strangers and Brothers* and has now been retitled *George Passant*. It recreates the hopeful, short-lived euphoria of Britain between the wars when most thinking people were liberals strongly committed to the freedom of the individual. The central character, George Passant, is a passionate fighter for freedom from restraint of all sorts, especially class and family. His faith in the perfectibility of the human individual and of the rewards that fulfilment can bring seem real to him, though tawdry enough to us who see it all from the vantage-point of history. He is the leader of a group of young people around him whom he fires with his enthusiasm. The self-delusion of the period and its wild hopefulness are well caught in the person of George. The *TLS* notes of George:

> ... [he is] a perfect example of the frustrated, talkative, provincial progressive of the twenties. Ten years earlier he could hardly have

existed; ten years later he would have been more openly political; he is placed in his time with the most loving sympathy.[13]

When George is on trial for fraud, his defence lawyer Herbert Getliffe seeks mercy for him because 'he represents a time and generation that is wretchedly lost by the side of ours',[14] and contrasts the earlier solidity with the fluid, anchorless twenties.

The Conscience of the Rich shows us the next decade seen through the eyes of the rich Anglo-Jewry. Mr March, with his backward-looking habit, is unwilling to allow the security of his little world to be broken up by the restless political ideas astir everywhere in Europe. Hearing the family stories of the Marches evoking a vanished world of security and comfort, Eliot feels a sort of homesickness for what he has never known. George Passant was unrealistically hopeful about the future; old Mr March is unrealistically nostalgic about the past; both refuse to recognise the tensions of the present. But Charles March does; his break with his family and fortune, while principally a study of individual freedom, is also to be seen as the awakening of the sick conscience of the rich when exposed to radical ideologies. He becomes a doctor in the poorer parts of London and marries Ann, a communist, representing the extreme left which was so vocal at that time in its agitation about the Civil War in Spain. Her intrusion into the family and the consequent splinterings show us a break-up that arises out of the political morality of the thirties.

It might be remarked here in passing that Helen Gardner is not much impressed by the Jewishness of Snow's Jewish family. In an otherwise highly appreciative article in the *New Statesman* she admits that his reflection is true but not revelatory; it sheds no new light:

> . . . although I am continually impressed by the truth and shrewdness of the comments on the habits and manners of wealthy Anglicized Jews, they are comments on a world I know already and do not know better for reading the book.[15]

There is a tricky problem here, for the Marches are on the surface completely assimilated but at the core tenacious about their Jewishness. There is little room, given such a family, to differentiate them sharply enough through external detail. Snow manages to convey an impression of something not quite Anglo-Saxon through Mr March's extraordinary conversation and total recall in which each detail is as important as any other. The exuberance and verve of his speech may be attributed to his Jewishness; it is very different from English phlegm. Apart from this, there is little save a mechanical mention or two to suggest that they are Jews in a Gentile world. Snow plays quite safe by Anglicising them.[16]

At the end of that decade comes the war. Snow has been criticised because he has two novels and a part of a third set in this period, and yet the presence of the war does not dominate any one of them. There is nowhere a full evocation of life in wartime. Yet I think he touches on the political divide in an obliquely effective way. In the novel *The Light and the Dark* there is an excellent picture of Germany just before the war: a Nazi officer supremely confident, and the ordinary, poor derelicts of society adrift and as untouched by official decisions as anywhere in the world till the disaster actually bursts upon them. Then in the last section of the book there is the actual war: fear, work, bombings, lives altered, the pressure and excitement, all briefly but effectively described. Within the stately home of the Boscastles the political quarrels become rougher; there is division within the family. The total disruption of the old tradition is brought home through the comments of Lady Boscastle. Old and frail, scrutinising her husband and son, she says with detachment that their day is done, perhaps it was already all over in 1914. Eliot muses on her strength to face change:

> She was far more detached than the rest of them about the fate of their world. She liked it; it suited her; it had given her luxury, distinction and renown; now it was passing forever, and she took it without a moan.[17]

Perhaps it might be said that beside the horror of the bombings, houses destroyed, flesh ripped, faces in the fire – beside all that, Eliot's comments on a vanishing world are ridiculously marginal and irrelevant. I think not. Through the deliberate conversation, the slight exchanges with their digressions and trivialities, a sense of loss and waste is conveyed indirectly and touchingly.

The book which deals most obviously with an important social theme is *The New Men*. Should the bomb be made? Once made, should it be used? The answer to the first question seems to be a qualified, hedged-about 'yes ... but ...'. The answer to the second question is an unequivocal 'no'. At the simplest level the book is significant because it deals with such an important and relevant contemporary theme. Bonamy Dobrée is quoted by Derek Stanford as admitting: 'Well, I suppose he (Snow) is important because he writes about those things which really matter.'[18]

This reluctant praise is perhaps most applicable to *The New Men*, which in many ways is unsatisfying as a novel but is of too much social relevance to ignore. Parts of it are excellently handled: the endless meetings of the scientists and the way they set about the refining of plutonium, for instance.

The horror of the bomb itself is so overwhelming that to play too much on it would have made for melodrama. Snow uses understatement instead. A fine example is his rendering of one of the most crucial moments in our history: news of the first atomic explosion over Hiroshima. Eliot has not heard the news. After a day of watching cricket he walks into a pub and there meets the literary critic-journalist who has just returned from giving a broadcast on 'Current Shakespeareana'. Eliot reports the scene thus:

> He said that he had had only one drink, but his bright, heavy face was glistening, he was talking as if he were half-drunk. 'And all the time I was thinking of my words going out to the villages and the country towns and clever young women saying: "That was a good point!" Or, "I should like to take that up with him." And then I came out of the studio and met the man who had been reading the six o'clock news just before I went on.' 'Is there any news?' I asked. 'There is,' said Hankins. 'So they've dropped it, have they?' I asked dully. I felt blank, tired out.[19]

Such a presentation of the disaster works because of its indirectness. To have presented it flat would have taken away the impact. The remarks of Hankins, upset and drunkenly hilarious, about the end of the party for 'dear old western man' convey the effect very impressively. Snow is realistic enough to note the toughness of human resilience; within minutes of the first numbing shock there are people in the pub who have thrown it off already. Eliot notices an elderly man with a fine ascetic face, his strained eyes fixed on the door, waiting for a young man who had been due at six. This is a good detail that tells us how few lose a night's sleep over the worst public disasters, but the pains and disappointments of the personal life strike at the nerve-ends.

The second and much longer part of *Homecomings* takes us into the fifties. It gives us a picture of Britain recovering her balance. After the intensity and trauma of the war years there is an emotional simmering down and the social mood has shifted to one of reconciliation, regularity and contentment. The Cold War clearly begins to cast its shadow but on the whole, life in Britain is approaching a new steadiness, reflected in the leisurely hum of bureaucracy so strongly present in this novel. There are numerous meetings, people to be interviewed, jobs to be filled, but the general tempo remains muted and unhurried. Snow reveals this new phase to the reader by showing us the inside of Whitehall, the to-and-fro-ing along the corridors. He has an uncanny feel for the early fifties which were politically quiet years for Britain with only a dim foreboding of things to come. Margaret's first husband, Geoffrey Hollis, is pictured as not bothering about political affairs. He does not even subscribe to a daily newspaper. Eliot comments:

> . . . this kind of quietism was becoming common among those I knew, and I distrusted it.[20]

In the novel *The Affair*, also set in this decade, a young don, Lester Ince, and his wife are politically committed to nothing at all. They do not even trouble to vote. How different this is from the radical fervour of young men twenty years earlier.

Economically, the size of Britain's cake was growing. The dream of the welfare state was slowly taking shape. Cold, hunger and disease were all being banished for the first time. Sidney Pollard remarks:

> The sense of material well-being, the assurance of economic progress to the point at which moralists began to deplore the prevailing materialism, and the absence of stirring social issues at home, became diffused among nearly all classes.[21]

Most of Britain went along with the political slogan that they 'had never had it so good'. This accounts for the undisturbed political and economic climate in which most of *Homecomings* is set.

Another new feature in this novel is the emergence of the industrialist who is prepared to invest large sums of money on scientific and technological research. Paul Lufkin, who seeks a government contract for manufacturing the hardware for the British Atomic Project at Barford, is such a figure. The war did a great deal to bring industry and government together; scientists and technologists assumed an important new role as originators of change and controllers of process. Pollard tells us that a total of about £300 million was spent on scientific research and development by private industry and government in 1955.[22] This novel shows the beginning of all that. Today, every big company maintains a Research and Development division; the government runs its own research laboratories; and there is lending and borrowing on both sides. That kind of coming together of government and industry is reflected in this novel.

In religious matters there was a new conservatism and piety and high Anglicanism came back with renewed force during this period. Tom Orbell and Julian Skeffington in *The Affair*, also set in the 1950s, are believers. Skeffington prays in chapel and goes to midnight mass on Christmas Eve; Orbell flaunts his piety at Eliot's expense. This faith is contrasted with the secular or agnostic leanings of people from an earlier generation. Old Arthur Brown, though conservative and Anglican, goes to the church 'out of propriety more than belief, and he was not entirely easy when young men like Orbell began displaying their religion'.[23]

By the end of that decade, the political divisions had hardened and the Cold War was a terrible reality. The possibility of total destruction through nuclear warfare looms over the most political of Snow's novels, *Corridors of Power*. Britain's dwindling status in world affairs and her helpless dependence on America, the nadir of British prestige in the post-war world touched during the Suez crisis – all this is reflected in the disarmament policy decided upon by Roger Quaife, a promising Conservative minister. He wants Britain to slide out of the arms race gradually, not merely because he is himself morally committed to peace, but more importantly because this makes the most political sense. He asks the famous American physicist, David Rubin, to tell him, in the crudest practical terms, how significant Britain's weapons are going to be.

'Well, if you must have it,' Rubin answered shrugging his shoulders, 'anything you can do doesn't count two per cent.'[24]

Later he advises Roger that this is not the right moment in history to go in for disarmament even if Britain's arms do not count for much. America needs Britain's moral support. Rubin continues:

But as of this moment, they're not all that interested in what you do – as long as you don't seem to be sliding out of the Cold War. This is the one thing that they're scared of. This is the climate.[25]

He firmly tells Roger Quaife that he is swimming against the tide; it would mean the end of his political life; and one valuable man would be wasted. The novel brings out very clearly both the fact of Britain's waning power as a military force and the climate thick with suspicion and mistrust. Whether Britain counts as a nuclear force or not, nerves are so frayed in the delicate business of keeping the balance of power that any radical step would be unacceptable. Whatever the facts may be, no one can afford to be too realistic and rational about them. The most realistic politician had better wait another ten years before Britain can start on such a course. Roger Quaife, of course, refuses to take this advice and pays the price. The humiliation felt by right-thinking Englishmen over the Suez invasion comes out in Eliot's angry remark: 'Countries, when their power is slipping away, are always liable to do idiotic things.'[26]

The *London Magazine* somewhat reluctantly acknowledged the authenticity of this novel:

The alacrity with which various Tory ministers leapt forward to denounce the book on its publication may well have prompted the malicious thought in some circles that its revelation of how government is actually conducted was too near the mark to be allowed to pass unnoticed.[27]

The 1960s saw material affluence reaching a peak in Britain. The slogan of that period was 'I'm all right, Jack'. The poor, old and sick were taken care of by the welfare state, and the young had never had it so good. But in 1967 the country was shaken by the ghastly Moors Murders in which two children and a youth were brutally tortured and killed by a young man and woman.[28] Many in the country felt that the Moors Murders were an extreme manifestation of the sickness of a society which had had too much of all it wanted. Great economic prosperity led to a change in sexual mores first recorded in *Corridors of Power* where divorces are depicted as common and people are as sexually tolerant as possible.[29] The Permissive Society, now here to stay for a long while yet, helped to nurture the idea that freedom means the freedom to do anything; fulfilment at any cost, however hideous and obscene. The clearest sign of Snow's preoccupation with social change is the fact that he dropped his plan of writing *The Devoted*, a novel which was to have dealt with a significant turn in Eliot's life. Instead, convulsed by the horror of the Moors Murders, and convinced that permissiveness was 'the earth out of which this poisonous flower grew', he wrote *The Sleep of Reason*.

The point made in this book is not that liberalism has vanished but that it has succeeded too well. George Passant, who had fought for freedom from poverty and inhibition for so long, finds it all of no avail and is left with an ashen taste in the mouth.[30] The dangerousness of George's faith in progress and human perfectibility is shown through the murderous behaviour of his disciples, his niece Cora Ross and her friend, Kitty Pateman. George had once sincerely fought for sexual freedom which in himself had degenerated into an old man's debased sensuality and the meetings of his Group into an excuse for cuddling girls. His influence on his niece and her friend was disastrous. The two girls, a lesbian pair, kidnap an eight-year-old boy, take him to a cottage, torture him, and eventually kill him, all as 'a sort of experiment. They wanted to see what it felt like'.[31] Together they had planned it all carefully, made fantasies about ultimate freedom, proud that they were breaking all rules, getting an obscene sexual satisfaction out of having a life at their mercy. Here is sexual freedom with a vengeance. On the whole, society in Britain is tolerant; permissiveness is well-established, but the question is: *where does one draw the line?* How far can permissiveness go?

Around this horror, Snow draws another picture from contemporary student life. Four students at a provincial university (one of them the brother of Kitty Pateman, one of the murderers) are expelled for having been caught in a sexual orgy in the women's hostel. The attitude of most of the university senate, except Arnold Shaw the Vice-Chancellor, is casual. Times have changed. Romantic notions about love are not so prevalent any more. Take your pleasure where you find it. Snow's attitude towards this is not especially denunciatory. He merely reflects the changes that have come about. But his intention is to awaken in society an awareness of the monsters that can leap forward once control and reason are altogether abandoned. Lewis Eliot is not much in sympathy with the puritanical Vice-Chancellor, but he *is* appalled by the lack of any rational control in the lives of the young.

The basic questions raised are: is this what Lewis Eliot has worked for? Is this the end to which the liberal faith leads one? Freedom has been achieved, but to what end? These are questions that go to the root of Eliot's whole way of life. Snow faithfully documents all his events, faintly hinting at the irony in the turn which history and social change have taken.

In *The Sleep of Reason* Snow presents the facts of the murder case as they are in a steadied tone of reason and restraint and without fully communicating to the reader the immense sense of horror inherent in the situation. The facts of the case, including the trial, psychiatrist's evidence, and so on, are presented with marvellous accuracy and without sensationalisation, but in the process evil tends to get smothered by the legal jargon and deliberate understatement. Snow does not attempt to dissect the immense complexity of characters like Cora Ross and Kitty Pateman; we see them entirely from the outside through the eyes of Sir Lewis Eliot, who never penetrates the heart of darkness to tell us what it is like from within.

However, in treating this crime, he has dealt with a subject that goes to the core of present-day society in the western world: once you have got your freedom and affluence what do you do with it? There is greater leisure, greater luxury; Cora Ross and Kitty Pateman can afford a car, record-player and records and various other comforts unthinkable in Eliot's youth in that same provincial town. But the 'better world' has not made for better human beings. The easy liberal piety about freeing the individual from deprivation to make him a more perfect human being is absurdly anachronistic in the context of this novel. Perhaps more hard work and less prosperity would have kept these two girls off their fantasies of ultimate freedom. This picture of modern society is contrasted rather effectively with the vanishing innocence of an earlier world through Eliot's father. As fumbling and mild as ever, tragedy strikes when the choir of which he is the secretary decides he is too old to work any more. His lack of sophistication, his determination to keep going independently to the very end and his refusal to take too readily to modern material comfort, stand distinctly apart from the rootlessness that too much affluence has brought. If in *Time of Hope* Lewis Eiot had hoped for a better world, in *The Sleep of Reason* he is not at all sure he has found it. From the sociological point of view this book, in my opinion, is one of the most significant.

The more attractive aspects of present-day youth are touched upon in the last book of the sequence, *Last Things*. Here the idealism and restiveness of bright young people, and their desire to improve the world in any way they can are presented through young Charles Eliot and his friends. Their purity of vision and intense humanitarianism impel them to launch an attack on a university which they suspect is doing research on biological warfare. *The Malcontents,* Snow's weakest novel, carries the dialogue with the young still further. The author comments here on the lack of ambition in modern youth and their casual and relaxed attitude about life in general. In some ways they are both more innocent than the previous generation (lacking passionate interest in success) and less so in others (efficiently organising strikes).

A light and charming illustration of Snow's grasp of the generation gap occurs in *Corridors of Power*. Francis Getliffe, distinguished scientist, professor at Cambridge, a stickler for formality and punctiliousness, has just had a letter from his daughter Penelope in the United States. He puts on his glasses and reads as though the language were Etruscan:

Dearest Daddy,

Please do not *flap*. I am *perfectly* alright, and perfectly happy, working like a beaver, and all is fine with Art and me, and we haven't any special plans, but he may come back with me in the summer – he isn't sure. There's no need for you to worry about us, we're just having a lot of fun, and nobody's bothering about marriage or anything like that, so do stop *questioning*. I think that you and Mummy must be *sex-maniacs*.

I have met a nice boy called Brewster (*first* name), and he dances as badly as I do so that suits us both. His father owns *three* night-clubs in Reno but I don't tell Art that!!! Anyway it is not at all serious and is only a bit of fun. I may go to Art's people for the weekend if I can raise the dollars. I don't always want him to pay for me.

No more now. Brew is fuming (much I care) because he's double-parked and says he'll get a ticket if I don't hurry. Must go.

Lots and Lots of love,
Penny

'Well,' said Francis, taking off his glasses. He broke out irritably, as though it were Penny's major crime: 'I wish she could spell *all right*.'[32]

Quite apart from the nice accuracy of tone there, the distance between generations is delightfully rendered.

Snow's latest novel, *In Their Wisdom*, shows us Britain in the seventies. We see her aware of her waning political power and ready to join the European Common Market. British society, having achieved sexual freedom, is preoccupied with money. The really poor figure nowhere perhaps because they no longer exist in the welfare states of Europe. Lord Lorimer, one of the poorest, teaches French at a day school and is really very comfortably off by the standards of the Third World. Lewis Eliot's childhood of poverty and the bankruptcy and economic disasters of *Time of Hope* seem very far away. It is 'big money' that fascinates now. Who will inherit the money? The estranged daughter left out of the will or the son of the dying man's secretary?

Enough has been said to show that Snow can handle almost any social situation and that his social nose is a very acute one. Lionel Trilling readily recognises this when he gives us a delightful imaginary re-construction of a scene in a club when Snow took a bet to write a novel which would show that the novel was not dead. Taking stock of his powers ('he did not have much to go on'), Trilling says that Snow does have a 'sense of social fact'.[33] David Lodge, in an article on jazz in the contemporary novel, notes with slight surprise that Snow has introduced a jazz fan into the stately combination-room of a Cambridge college, and remarks:

> Sir Charles Snow is no fan himself, one imagines, but he can recognize a new social type when he sees it, and in *The Affair* (1960) the Cambridge college of *The Masters* is brought up to date by the introduction of Lester Ince.[34]

The shift from solitary, private concerns to public and social issues has not been a bad thing for the novel, and Snow has been one of the earliest to attempt a balance between the two. However, Angus Wilson warns:

> ... while the novel of sensibility can become a poor substitute for poetry, so the social novel may be a vehicle for statements better and more economically made in the form of intelligent sociological articles. A more serious defect, I believe, lies in the sacrifice of depth of vision for that breadth of setting which is essential to what I have called 'adult statement'.[35]

In the case of Snow's fiction, while any single novel may seem in parts to have spilled over into documentary journalism, viewed all together they afford an impressive view of twentieth-century life.

I do not believe that Snow puts greater value on the social scene than on the private life. But I do believe that he does the social scene better. Perhaps that is why the social aspect of the novels leaves a lasting impression. In a leading article entitled 'What is a Novel' the *TLS* says:

> One very important thing that a novel can do (and it is hard to see that any other literary form can do it in the same way) is to help us assess the daily tone or timbre of life . . .[36]

Snow has assessed this daily tone or timbre with remarkable closeness. The cumulative effect at the end of the *Strangers and Brothers* sequence is that one has learned what it was like to live in England during those years; what ordinary life felt like; how people coped with crises both private (a love affair gone wrong) and public (Hitler and Hiroshima). The hum and buzz of life are there all right though rendered more unflurried by the even tone of the narrator. The relevant details – Eliot's father disgraced, a faded photograph of his mother in better days, animated faces in George's group, old Mr March's obsessive locking-up for the night, the clash of voices and tempers as Eliot and Calvert argue about Nazi Germany, Sheila's total indifference on the night of Munich, the bombing raids in which Calvert dies, the news about Hiroshima, the quiet evening at Douglas Osbaldistone's, the 'circling courtesies' of Hector Rose, walnuts and wine after dinner at Cambridge, Ministers spending weekends in country houses, industrialists throwing dinner parties, students striking and fornicating, the record-player in the front room where Kitty Pateman and Cora Ross live, young Charles Eliot walking in the rain after his first experience of love, ageing sick peers in the House of Lords, the vote on the Common Market – one has lived through fifty years because of details such as these. No sociological article could ever give us the *feel* of the time in this manner. While Snow considers matters beyond political and historical reckoning, he is firmly rooted in his cultural environment. This has value in an age in which we have, in Malcolm Bradbury's phrase, 'turned on to literature a more sociological eye'.

3 The examined life

While Snow gets the correct social setting in his novels, it is for him only the external layer. He has a good documentary eye and sharp sense for any currents afloat in the air, but his main interests are the human being functioning within society and the examination of human characters in search of a meaningful code. A morally examined life is central to most novels by Snow. If F. R. Leavis had not been so outraged by the semi-philistinism he thought Snow stood for and had read at least four or five novels by Snow without prejudgement, he would have found them permeated by moral concern. Leavis, who reproached the Bloomsbury group for not being moral enough, condemned Snow for not being sufficiently aesthetic in his response to life.

Admittedly Snow's denunciation of the literary tradition in the *Two Cultures* lecture was somewhat unfortunate in its lack of qualifications; there the tone was a bit too sweeping and betrayed an absence of aliveness to nuance. This defect, however, is not discernible in the novels, where the bland and generalising tone of the lectures is seldom heard. Instead, there is full recognition of hesitation, conflict, and many other possible responses as through the lives of his characters Snow poses and ponders over such questions as: how does one live as decently as one can? What values should one live by? The answers that emerge from these novels with their emphasis on integrity and self-knowledge have, it seems to me, a great deal of moral significance. Helen Gardner concludes in an article on Snow:

> . . . the whole enterprise seems to me the most impressive attempt in our generation to explore through fiction the moral nature of man.[1]

As much as the heroes of modernist novels Snow's central characters are in search of identity, but they find it in entirely different ways. In most cases they strive to come to terms with the world in which they live through different degrees of compromise. Among those who are failures

33

in doing this are Roy Calvert, Sheila Knight and George Passant. Among those who arrive at some partial workable solution are Lewis Eliot, Charles March and, outside the *Strangers and Brothers* sequence, Arthur Miles. Still others desire or seek no such compromise and deliberately set themselves a harsh choice between success and the abstract ideal. Such men are Martin Eliot and Roger Quaife.

The waifs of the world, the lost and wandering, are those who, with all their inborn gifts, refuse to settle down and feel at home in society. Eliot's first wife, Sheila, and his closest friend, Roy Calvert, are both such isolated and unhappy people. It is interesting to see that the young Eliot, for all his faith in reason and will, is drawn most intimately to these two, who have not a shred of conviction about either. They are both shown as cases verging on mental breakdown. Sheila Knight tends towards depressive withdrawal. Roy Calvert has a touch of the manic, with wild alternating cycles of gaiety and despair.

Sheila wants desperately to do good and love someone and she spends large chunks of her income on lame ducks who need money, but nothing gives her peace. There is a brilliant account of a man called Robinson in *Homecomings*, a practised, charming rogue who borrows her money and then spreads scandal about her. She marries Eliot without loving him because she is not strong enough to go on alone. Not surprisingly, Eliot's interest in worldly success is something which she hardly recognises; it has no meaning for her: 'It seemed to her empty and my craving for success vulgar.'[2] Comfortless and 'splintered', and with little contact with reality, she finally commits suicide.

Roy Calvert, the hero of *The Light and the Dark,* has magical charm and elegance. Besides, at the age of twenty-seven, he is an Oriental scholar with a European reputation. But he is subject to attacks of *accidie* and melancholy and is frequently so overwhelmed that he sees no point in carrying on. Even his work is an escape from despair; the love of women does nothing to assuage it. By temperament religious, what he hopes for is faith in God but science and the enlightenment have effectively made that impossible. As in the case of Sheila, fame and success have no meaning, and like her, he too is driven to death. He joins the most dangerous flying missions during the war and dies in a blaze when his aircraft is shot down.

Roy Calvert has been presented by Snow as an existential hero for whom social confrontation is neither desirable nor possible. I do not believe that Snow has contempt for such figures. He says in the *REL* interview:

I am probably more deeply interested in failure than I am in success. Anyone who knows the novels as well as you do will realise that in fact the characters I am most profoundly concerned with are not the people who ride their lives easily. I mean George Passant, Calvert, Charles March and so on.[3]

In creating Roy Calvert, Snow has, however, attempted something totally untypical of him. Roy's emotional range is wider than Eliot's.
Capable of ecstasy and hopelessness, he is Snow's 'black' hero in search
of God. This is the nearest Snow comes to presenting the dilemma
which is traditionally the stuff of literature, man's fate or destiny in an
ultimate sense. He does not succeed in this as well as in his portrayals of
men in their more ordinary roles, but here, I believe, he comes closest to
showing his awareness of the transcendent, or at least man's need for the
transcendent. The loving care he expends on Roy Calvert clearly shows
the fascination that this sort of temperament has for him. In fact he
exaggerates Roy Calvert's charm, elegance and style to the point of
making him too much of a cliché and, given his gloom, Roy emerges as
an astonishingly Byronic[4] figure.

Roy makes no effort whatever to fit into society; life as we ordinarily
live it is unreal to him. He hardly cares whether he is elected as a Fellow
of his college or gets the recognition he knows is his by right. While his
friends, Eliot, the master Vernon Royce and Colonel Ffoulkes, the
Oriental historian, take care of these matters for him, Roy observes the
goings-on with detachment almost amounting to indifference.

The difference between Everyman and Roy Calvert is explicitly
recognised by the narrator.

> Most men, I thought, are content to stay clamped within the bonds of
> their conscious personality. They may break out a little – in their
> daydreams, their play, sometimes in their prayers and their thoughts
> of love. But in their work they stay safely in the main stream of
> living. They want success on the ordinary terms, they scheme for
> recognition, titles, position, the esteem of solid men. They want to go
> up step by step within their own framework.[5]

Ordinarily Snow is content to have his heroes find their meaning within
an ordinary stream of living. Lewis Eliot, Arthur Miles, even Charles
March manage to do this in various degrees. They break out a little, as
he says, but they do not struggle to free themselves of social nets entirely. Snow has been so much regarded as the worldly writer, the creator of
the professional man, that I think the other side of him, his absorption
with failures, has gone either unnoticed or understressed; wanhope is
not dismissed by Snow; it is in fact viewed with sympathy and understanding though not with a sense of participation. Eliot and Calvert
are very intimate but very different, a fact that puzzles Calvert:

> So much of our sense of life we had in common: he could not easily or
> willingly accept that it led me to different fulfilments, even to different
> despairs. Most of all, he could not accept that I could get along with
> fairly even spirits, and not be driven by the desperate needs that took
> hold of him in their ineluctable clarity.[6]

Eliot, till well on into old age, can be comforted by reason and the shared socially useful life; only the terror of death at the end unnerves him. Even after that he carries on fairly steadily, shaken, more isolated, but able to come back to society and again be involved. Snow sees involvement and adjustment as one possible way of living a life of order and meaning.

Snow's view of character is fairly deterministic. He believes that there are parts of our nature which are unalterable or too heavy to shift, a core which we carry along with us from birth to death. For Calvert, given his nature, nothing can help or shape, for from the beginning he has felt excluded from the mercy of God. What possible interest can society hold for him after that conviction? Eliot's own understanding of life is enriched and widened because of his friendship with Roy Calvert. His own 'idiot hope' carries him through, but he watches with anguish while Roy sinks and fails.

It would be a mistake to interpret Roy Calvert as simply a symbol of the late thirities on the verge of a war. He is the only person in Snow's many novels who is an embodiment of 'the last naked him',[7] the one person raising unanswerable questions. For most of the other people in the novels these questions do not exist. By a few, like Eliot, they are heard, but not allowed to become too persistent, for they might stand in the way of the limited good they are capable of doing. Social usefulness, 'attempting to wipe out some of the revocable suffering and poverty in the world',[8] is recognised as a praiseworthy, modest goal. To ask 'then what?', as people like Roy Calvert might do, is not very health-giving, for it might prevent the chances of doing any good at all. This is perhaps the reason why Snow has skirted these ultimate issues after *The Light and the Dark* though he returns to them in *Last Things*.

George Passant, the central figure of the novel now bearing that name (originally called *Strangers and Brothers*), is another failure, a man who thinks he is clear about what he wants from life, lives it out deludedly and exuberantly at first, and dies a broken man, far from home. His championship of personal liberty links him, strangely enough, to a violent and obscene crime. Though he lacks personal ambition he inspires many in the group of which he is the leader; he gives them glimpses of a life much more intense than they dreamed of in their dull, middling rounds; he talks about the perfectibility of man in a way that holds their imagination. The old liberal piety – free a man from poverty and chains and leave him free to live as he likes – is George's article of faith.

But the seeds of personal tragedy lie dormant in George's lack of self-knowledge. He fails to see that, as time goes on, the meetings of his group are becoming charged with an increasingly fervent sexual temperature; that his own sensual nature is taking over. In such an atmosphere, his repeated insistence on freedom – and George means

sexual as much as political and economic freedom – has a corrupting influence. He gets involved in a financial deal based on fraud and is
acquitted after a trial. After a stint with Eliot in the Civil Service (he is
judged too odd and uncontrolled, however brilliant, to be permanently
retained), he returns to his job as a clerk in his old firm of solicitors.
George's progress downhill towards drink and degradation is carefully
traced through the series. He stumbles in and out of the later novels, his
physical running to seed indicative of the inner debasement. George's
spirit, after the murder trial of his niece and her friend (once part of his
group), is finally crushed. He leaves the town, a fat seedy old man,
though still loved by his friends.

George, who started out convinced of the truth of his ideal, failed to
see what he was becoming because he was not 'in touch with his own
experience' and lacked strength of will. In the trial for fraud his lawyer
gets him off on the plea that the breakdown of tradition has thrown up
people like George who might end up doing a fair amount of harm in
the mistaken name of idealism. George is indignant and resentful that
he should be thus explained away but the explanation is largely true.
George *is* a product of the inter-war period. His movement towards personal freedom was in itself a fine ideal, but it took more responsibility
and awareness of limits than George could bring to achieve it. Bernard
Bergonzi is surely wrong when, after describing George as 'unusually
able and intelligent, idealistic and at the same time boorish with strong
physical passions', he goes on to say: 'Yet the whole intention of the
novel is that we should see Passant as more than just this.'[9]

Quite the contrary. We are meant to see George as *just that*: a failed
leader; able, yes, but held back by physical weaknesses and mental
blindness. His brief appearances in the later books gradually build up
an ineradicable impression – the over-hearty shouts, the fixed anxious
questions, the unfocused stare. Eventually what happens in *The Sleep of
Reason* is not a total shock.

George does not aspire for much in his job. He does most of his
firm's work with great competence, often brilliance. But it never occurs
to him that he can step upward into anything better, just as it had never
occurred to him after leaving school that, with his academic record, he
could get a university scholarship. In his firm he takes it for granted that
he will eventually be made a partner, and when Eden does not make him
one, he accepts that too. What is responsible for George's failure in
terms of personal development is basically his lack of discipline. If he
had had enough discipline to renounce the world and success as Martineau does, or as even Eliot's brother does to some extent, then he
would not have failed. With more self-control he could have been the
leader of a more meaningful group, had more material success (which
he would have liked) and he could then have kept off the unsavoury
odour that gathers about him as he ages. He can marshal a legal argu-

ment with great clarity, but he cannot apply his reasoning intelligence to
the ordering of his inner life, for he has not examined it sufficiently. A
lack of introspective knowledge carries him down.

Roy Calvert and George Passant are both failures but for opposite
reasons. Roy sinks under too much introspection; his ability to act is im-
paired by too much thought. George sinks because he is not sufficiently
introspective, not honest with himself. He fails to examine his intentions
scrupulously enough. There is no poise within George; even his wish to
free society from its inhibitions is seen to be an outcome of his strong
sensual nature not properly understood. His rages against the
successful, self-righteous 'sunkets' or 'bellwethers' of high society (his
terms) arise from a deep-seated complex of social inferiority, not
knowing which fork to use in polite society. Likewise, his urging the
young people to cut family ties and live as fully as they can arises from
his own unbridled passions. Both Lewis and Martin Eliot acknowledge
that George, at an important period in their lives, gave them a sense of
the largeness of life, and they are his friends till the end. But they out-
grow him quickly. He has set out plans for society before he has
governed himself; but he that ruleth his spirit is better than he that
taketh a city.

Roy Calvert cannot rule his spirit any better than George Passant in
spite of expending all his energies on that pursuit. Mandel and
Hamilton, in different articles in the *Queen's Quarterly*, make two opposite conclusions. Mandel says that Snow is contemptuous of an individual like Roy Calvert who is concerned with his own moral nature.[10]

Hamilton argues that Snow has no contempt even for the individual
who opposes social values in the name of private good, as in *The Search*.[11]

Mandel's word 'contempt' is, I believe, much too strong for Snow's
attitude of understanding. I admit that in his lectures Snow is more un-
qualified in his disapproval of the narcisstic individual, but the Snow of
the novels is far more tolerant and open-minded. The temperament of
the lecturing Snow, the public sage, is different from that of Snow the
novelist; the latter is more sensitive, as stated in the opening of this
chapter, to the personal life. I believe that he neither condemns Roy
Calvert's obsession with final things nor holds it up as especially ad-
mirable. In fact, it is clear that Eliot is made to feel a sympathy for Roy
strong enough to be called love. When Roy ruefully observes that Eliot's
life would have been happier if he, Roy, had never lived, Eliot replies:

> 'Never mind about happiness,' I said. 'It can cut one off from too
> much. My life would have been different without you. I prefer it as it
> is.'[12]

Roy Calvert himself knew, says Eliot, that any profound friendship must
contain a little of the language of love. Elsewhere, Eliot, walking with
Roy, is moved strongly enough to reflect:

. . . And at the same moment that I felt closer to him than I had ever done, I was seized and shaken by the most passionate sense of his nature, his life, his fate. It was a sense which shook me with wonder, fear and pity, with horror and unassuageable anxiety, with wonder, illumination and love. I accepted his nature with absolute gratitude; but I could not accept how fate had played with him and caught him . . . I cried to myself with the bitterness of pity; to know him was one of the two greatest gifts of my life; and yet it was anguish to see how his life had brought him to this point.[13]

If this, as Peter Fison says, is not the language of love, what else can it be called? The point to be made is that Roy Calvert is not treated with contempt because he is unable to come to terms with life. Both he and Sheila Knight, however, are regarded as being on the fringe of mental illness. Isolation of that sort leads nowhere. While Eliot is fully sympathetic to such people, he himself regards adjustment to society, the harmonising of outer and inner, as crucial to the growth of a human being. Roy Calvert and George Passant are failures because they lack moderation or balance which, Snow implies, is the healthful way out of life's traps. On the other hand, we might feel that Lewis Eliot, who strikes a balance between the excesses of Roy and George, is colourless and complacent and essentially mediocre. To one who holds that compromise is the death of the soul he will seem to be all these things. But if one recognises the difficulty of making simple black-and-white choices in today's complex competitive life, then Lewis Eliot for all his bloodlessness emerges as a fair representative of the contemporary hero.

In Snow's earliest novel, *The Search,* Arthur Miles is presented as a man who tries to strike a balance between the social and private good. He is a brilliant research scientist who has done excellent research work on crystals and is dreaming of becoming the head of a biophysics institute. Devoted as he is to science, he becomes involved with handling people, an adept at committees, highly gifted, but by no means a genius. This is brought home by the contrast of his very considerable talents with the gifts of another scientist, Constantine, who is in fact a genius, but by nature wild and uncontrollable. Arthur Miles suffers by comparison. A growing understanding of his own limitations is the beginning of the end of his science. It takes him a long time to realise it; he still wants the power that the headship of the institute can give; he works for it with patience and cunning; it is almost in his hands. Then a piece of research goes wrong. Without checking the data provided by his assistant, he confidently publishes his result and is quickly challenged. The timing of this is disastrous as it happens just before the directorship of the institute is decided, and it then goes to another man. Miles is offered instead the post of assistant director.

In sections four and five of Chapter 8 in the third part of the novel, Miles puts himself through a rigorous self-examination.[14] Bitterly disappointed by his failure, Miles is honest enough, after considerable soul-searching, to face the truth that he really had no devotion to science. So that it may not look as if he is leaving science because of pique over his failure, he swallows his pride and works for three years as hard as he can under Tremlin, re-establishes his reputation and then leaves. He plans now to write because he realises that human intricacies absorb him more totally than scientific facts.

The important point to be taken is that hard will and the reasoning power can cope with many sorts of obstacle. Starting as a poor young man, Miles had made his way into Cambridge. And now, after his fresh start as a writer, he is able to find a new meaning in life. Once that meaningfulness is identified, the world outside can be manipulated. However, the inner struggle to find this meaning is harder; it demands humility and self-knowledge and the facing of disturbing truths. Miles has known the joy of successful scientific research. To find a new identity through defeat, to recognise that one's vocation is other than what one had thought, to give up joy and start anew – this is a theme that Snow deals with repeatedly in his later novels. *The Search* is not a very satisfying novel as a whole, but this particular theme in it is handled with sureness.

When Miles decides to rebuild his position by working fiercely at science before giving it up, he plays safe with the committee to make sure he will get the assistant directorship. To do this he has to sacrifice a friend whom he had earlier planned to take into the institute. When he withdraws his case for Sheriff (a somewhat disreputable friend of college days), the committee is placated. They interpret it as an apology for all the reckless, arrogant gestures of his youth:

> I was becoming tamed, they felt; as always, the respectabilities were winning in the end.[15]

He is left with a slightly ashen taste in the mouth after compromising, but he has to come to terms with the world around him. To make futile gestures from an isolated height does not help much. To mature is to compromise. There is awareness of loss, but this is adulthood.

After three years of hard work and a fresh scientific reputation, Arthur Miles leaves the institute, marries, and takes to writing. He also helps his friend Sheriff along on his erratic scientific career to some degree of success by privately guiding his research. Sheriff then takes up one of Miles's abandoned scientific projects against his advice, 'cooks' the result and publishes it without telling Miles, in the hope of being appointed to a vacant chair at a university. When Miles reads the paper, he knows from his own experience that there is one point at which Sheriff must have falsified the data to get the neat result he did.

What should Miles do? He writes a letter to the journal in which Sheriff has published his paper but, knowing the difference it will make to his friend's career, he cannot bring himself to send it off. He knows that not to send it would mean breaking irrevocably with science, thereby closing the retreat he had till then left open to himself:

> It was twenty years and more ago, I thought, that night when my scientific passion first broke hot upon me; and, through curiosity, satisfaction, ecstasy, strenuous work, a career, disaster, recovery, partial severance, I had come to this. The passion was over now. I lit a match and put it to the corner of the letter; the flame was steady in the still air, golden and smoky-edged. The passion was over. I had repudiated it, and I should never feel it again.[16]

The human and personal values win out in the struggle during which Miles has recognised a truth beyond that of the scientific order. For him to have sent that letter in a flush of self-righteousness, after being fully aware of the human issues involved, would have been slightly Pharisaic. Fellow-feeling, even to the point of allowing a minor fraud to pass, is more important than a personal sense of justification at having done the right thing. For what is the right thing anyway? He can lie low and say nothing till someone finds out his friend's 'mistake'. By that time Sheriff would be sure of his chair, and could explain it all away with his persuasive charm.

A complex moral dilemma is raised here though Snow does not analyse it in the novel. Should people like Sheriff (eloquent, voluble, but feckless and not over-scrupulous) be allowed to occupy positions of responsibility? If Miles, by not acting at once, is allowing this to happen, how responsible and reliable a member of society is he himself? Where do charity and tolerance begin or end? Can tolerance be made to include wrongdoing?

By implication all these questions are raised by Arthur Miles's decision in the last two pages of the book. Though Snow does not answer them, one concludes that one has to settle for oneself what truth means and act according to one's conscience in the light of that. As to allowing Sheriff a responsible post, he has been throughout portrayed as mercurial and unquestionably intelligent, a man of much attractiveness but not much staying-power. In spite of his slight dishonesty Sheriff would never have the courage for major wrongs. Success might be good for him; a professorship might give him stability; and he is not much worse than many others in such places. Between him and Desmond, a professor at Oxford and a Fellow of the Royal Society, there is not much to choose. Both are of the same tribe and success alone divides them; if anything, Desmond is the more practised rogue. These are perhaps not very good reasons for helping to elect a man to a full professorship, but they are also not strong enough arguments for holding him down.

In *The Conscience of the Rich* Charles March feels the need to find his own way in life independent of the expectations of his enormously rich Jewish Family. They expect him to become a lawyer in the family tradition; to marry a girl out of their own wealthy circle; to live the life of the wealthy Anglo-Jews, conservative in politics, upholding their own class-system and undisturbed by the restlessness of Britain in the nineteen-thirties. The issue is complicated by old Mr March's fierce possessiveness; he wants for his son the brilliant career he himself never had. It appears that Charles March is reacting against three factors, all interwoven: his Jewish background, his family tradition and his father's possessive love. The pain of being Jewish is suggested by Charles March's initial refusal to talk about his family and by the reluctance of both Charles and his sister Katherine to attend Jewish Friday night dances. The reaction against family tradition and demanding parental affection is seen in his capricious giving up of law after he is fully qualified as a lawyer and in his marrying the radical Ann Simon whom his father considers a pernicious influence even though he is himself strangely attracted to her. For a long time after he has abandoned law Charles March just drifts, unhappy and restless, not satisfied with any of the alternatives open to him, for they are 'all pretty frivolous'. Lewis Eliot comments:

> I ought also to have known that he wanted to lead a useful life. He could not confide it or get rid of it, but he had a longing for the good.[17]

Eventually he qualifies as a doctor and sets up practice in a poor neighbourhood even at the risk of being cut out of his father's will. His daily round and common task are pretty drab but his nature has been tranquillised and he has found his individual freedom. Eliot puts down Charles's abnegation partly to the radical faith of his time and partly to his inner struggle against his own guilty and sadistic nature.

But the novel does not end here. Though Charles has found the meaning of personal freedom, will he, under stress, respect the freedom of another? This is tested some years after his marriage. Charles's wife Ann works for a communist weekly called *The Note* which spreads scandal about the government in power. One of the ministers involved is Philip March, Mr March's elder brother and head of the March clan. The present scandal is based on falsehood, but Philip March's earlier financial transactions happen not to have been so innocent. *The Note* threatens to use the scandal of many years ago to give credibility to a lie for its own political purposes. It is in Ann's power to stop the weekly altogether as she has in her hands its private papers which are sufficiently incriminating to cause its suppression if the authorities can get them. She does what she can to avert disgrace. She pleads with the editor not to falsify the information and is flatly turned down. What she can do now is to use her own knowledge about *The Note* to get it suppressed. Immense family pressure is brought upon Charles to force her hand and ruin the paper, thus reneging the cause to which she is committed. Charles himself is politically not at all committed to Ann's faith and he doubts the usefulness of journalism of the kind practised by the *Note*. But he refuses to try and influence his wife. Her beliefs are her beliefs; having fought for his own freedom he will not curtail another's even if it means disgrace to the Marches. There is a scene with his sister Katherine who asks how it can possibly matter if he seeks to persuade Ann. He replies:

> Simply that this is something Ann believes in. The suggestion is that I should force her to betray it.[18]

To which his sister comes back with:

> You must be mad . . . You can't give us a better reason than that for getting Uncle Philip into the newspapers.[19]

To all of them Charles's behaviour seems fantastically delicate, much too idealised and remote to have any bearing on the present crisis. Can devotion to an ideal be so strong that it will allow the family name to be disgraced? She urges him:

> If your marriage is worth anything at all, this can't make any difference. Don't you see that you can't afford to be too considerate? And we can't afford to let you be. Could anyone in the world think the reason you've given is enough excuse for ruining Mr. L's peace of mind for the rest of his life?[20]

But Charles refuses to give in. The scandal is published, has its effect and Philip March loses his job. Now the break with his family is complete. His father asks him in bitterness and defeat why he had found it necessary to act as he had done, why he had been compelled to break every connection with the family.

The story of Charles March's search for meaning ends on a positive note. He may be poorer and disowned but he has established a meaningful relationship with society through his work, and harmonised his emotional life through his marriage. This is a novel based on the favourite Snow thesis that, given a strong enough will, reasonableness and self-knowledge, one can achieve a fair adjustment with life. Compromise and sacrifice may be necessary but there is some increase, though never very much, in peace of mind.

The main strands in the pattern of Lewis Eliot's life can be readily summarised: ambitious pursuit of success and love; frustrations and defeats followed by joyous fulfilment in career and marriage; a continuous adjustment between the outer and inner life leading, after many trials of the spirit and flesh, to a certain equilibrium and poise which is shaken but survives the confrontation with death; finally a gradual disillusionment but a stoic acceptance of the world.

This pattern is worked out in three books: *Time of Hope*, *Homecomings* and *Last Things*, which together form a cycle tracing the growth of Eliot from boyhood to old age. The first book shows the strength of Eliot's drives both towards success and defeat. In his profession he stakes all he has on one big gamble, never resting till he wins. Simultaneously he marries Sheila Knight and finds the marriage draining away his reserve of energy because of her mental instability and inability to reciprocate his love. Their relationship is sustained for a time by the curious inner satisfaction he derives from his suffering for her sake, but finally he breaks down. He faces a painful but honest self-appraisal in much the same way as Arthur Miles had done in *The Search*:

> I had longed for a better world, for fame, for love. I had longed for a better world; and this was the summer of 1933. I had longed for fame; and I was a second-rate lawyer. I had longed for love; and I was bound for life to a woman who had never had love for me and who had exhausted mine.[21]

Lewis Eliot's will for success is frustrated by forces not in his control. The world outside himself, which he usually feels can be controlled by will, is at this time heading towards war and there is little he can do about it. The world within is as little to be manipulated by reason though he recognises the forces that have driven him to his own emotional traps of defeat. This must be what he had wanted, even if it makes him wretched at the level of conscious existence. Snow says in his biographical sketch of Einstein:

> But – much more than we think in our rationalisations – what you want is what happens to you.[22]

That is, will operates at a deeper level than the rational; we are largely responsible for our fates, for our emotional lives at any rate.

The novel *Homecomings* shows Eliot's growth towards fulfilment and harmony which come to him partly from his job as a civil servant. He is happy working with people in committees and watching human reactions with curiosity. But he also needs to find serenity and joy in the private, emotional life, which he ultimately discovers when Margaret Davidson agrees to marry him by breaking up her own stable marriage with Geoffrey Hollis, by whom she has had a child. The sacrifice from her which Eliot demands is presented by Snow as a sign of Eliot's need and readiness for a more satisfying emotional fulfilment than he has had with Sheila Knight. This morality of self-fulfilment at any price is somewhat questionable and curious. As Margaret Davidson says of her first husband:

> He's never done a thing to me . . . that isn't as considerate as it could be. He's not given me a single bad hour to hold against him. How can I go to him and say 'Thank you, you've been good to me, now for no reason that I can possibly give you I intend to leave you cold?'[23]

Snow's faith in romantic love is so strong that it outweighs other moral considerations altogether. Before Eliot's first marriage to Sheila Knight, when Sheila is trembling on the verge of happiness with another young man, he drives away her lover by warning him that Sheila is mentally unstable. The message is that, where love is concerned, one has to be completely egotistical and ruthless. In the emotional life one's first responsibility is to oneself. Romantic love is not softened or sentimentalised; it is shown as harsh and self-involved, but it is the fulfilment at the heart of existence and no price is too high. Once this joyous relationship has been established, Eliot is serene in his private world and can afford to be concerned about more public issues like disarmament, student unrest and the affluent and permissive society.

Taking up social responsibility henceforward becomes a major theme in his life. He explicitly says that though there are always fine, sensitive reasons for 'contracting out' of social involvement, it can leave you dead. So in *The Affair*, irritably, half against his will, he lets himself be drawn into a reinvestigation of a case of possible injustice. In the early novel *Strangers and Brothers* he goes down to help George at his trial for fraud in spite of utter wretchedness with Sheila. In *The Sleep of Reason* he postpones an eye-operation (where delay may mean partial loss of vision) because he is urgently needed at a University meeting, and later in the novel does not shrink from the glare of publicity that is turned on to George as uncle of one of the murderers. Since Eliot is a well-known name by now in some circles his support of George through this final horror, despite the full newspaper coverage, is a sign of Eliot's full understanding of the word brotherliness. All this, when thus baldly set down, may sound like a facile theory of good works, but knowing the stresses of Eliot's life, it is not as easy as it seems. Snow suggests that life in society can be invigorating, but only after the inner emotional life has been tranquillised in a love-relationship. After Eliot's marriage to Margaret Davidson, there are few storms within.

Radiating from Eliot's inner peace is his tolerance for human weakness and concern for human life. He had always had a 'forbidding' interest in power but, as we see from *Last Things*, once he has held some sort of it in his hands, he learns to put it in its proper place. I believe that Snow, through Eliot, wants to give us a picture of a man both of action and contemplation. Eliot, even in the thick of affairs, is capable of introspective insight. He is a man in and of the world but not a self-satisfied prig. That, I believe, is as far as Snow goes.

Critics have charged that Lewis Eliot is, first, not a very good man, and second, far too complacent. It is Rayner Heppenstall who says, 'I am not altogether sure that he is a good man'.[24] He says this because Eliot is so politic, so adept at speaking the right word in the right ear. That sort of prudence, for Heppenstall, rules out heroism and is antithetical to goodness. The first question to be raised about this charge is:

why *should* he be a totally good man? Surely every interesting central character in fiction and drama has been a mixture of good and bad; it is precisely that which makes character interesting. If, on the other hand, by good Heppenstall means magnanimous and selfless and capable of the heroic gesture, it is true, of course, that Eliot seems to lack these qualities. But this is not to say that Eliot has no appreciation of the word 'goodness'. He is not indifferent to power and success but the ethical dilemma, the question of moral choice, is a preoccupation with him. Nor is it true, as Rabinovitz has charged, that he 'equates the idea of goodness with success'.[25] He neither shrugs off worldly claims nor puts them highest. He represents the virtue which has sallied out into the thoroughfares of the world and which has seen and known and yet abstained from the ultimate soul-destroying compromises. Eliot has his share of success but when the issue he believes in most firmly is overwhelmingly thrown out (nuclear disarmament, in *Corridors of Power*), he does bow out of the official world. He has sufficient sense of decency to do that. In the word 'decency', I believe, lies the contemporary notion of honour and goodness. It may sound drab by the side of the soaring, golden sacrifices, but it is authentic and touching. Eliot's struggle to maintain even decency and integrity is essentially a moral struggle, endowing him with a peculiar, quiet goodness.

Rabinovitz remarks that Lewis Eliot is smug and complacent and too much given to name-dropping, self-congratulation and snobbery.[26] True enough, Eliot enjoys his success, but not, I believe, to the point where he ceases to examine himself. Here is Eliot on the subject of his own rise:

> Working under me for nearly two years of war, Gilbert had seen me promoted; he had his ear close to the official gossip. He magnified both what I had done and what was thought of it, but it was true enough that I had made in some powerful anonymous *couloirs*, some sort of reputation. Partly I had been lucky, for anyone as close to the Minister as I was could not help but attract attention: partly, I had immersed myself in the job, with no one to watch over, no secret home to distract me.[27]

One cannot really lay the charge of smugness or complacency to this honest self-appraisal when Eliot explicitly attributes the cause of his success to factors other than his ability.

Rabinovitz goes on to point out Eliot's sense of his own 'moral superiority' on the grounds that he speaks contemptuously of Roy Calvert's and George Passant's amorous escapades and of Hanna Puchwein's suspected unfaithfulness.[28] This, it seems to me, is a wrong reading of the novels. As I read it, not only is that contempt just not there but, in fact, something like the opposite is present. Eliot is extremely sympathetic to people who are in pursuit of a sexual haven.

Throughout his life Eliot keeps his humility and sense of shared humanity. Speaking of a friend's love of gossip he says:

> I knew better than he thought; for in my youth I had been as tempted
> as most men by the petty treachery, the piece of malice warm on the
> tongue at a friend's expense.[29]

These are not words of a man blinded by self-righteousness. Eliot may
compromise frequently and show harsh and unlikeable traits, but he
manages to keep his awareness and honesty.

The sketch of Martineau in *Strangers and Brothers* is an illustration of
Snow's fondness also for the world-renouncing type. When he is in his
fifties Martineau turns religious, not in a conventional, church-going
sense but in a much more deeply felt, eccentric and evangelical way. He
literally gives up all he has and follows Christ, sleeping on pavements,
preaching, disappearing from all comforting routine and yet remaining
cheerful and carefree. He tries to throw off the burden of self as much as
he can, sometimes in the oddest possible way. For instance, he gives
away his share in the firm to his partner Eden. When Eliot tries to persuade him to give it to George (of whom Martineau is very fond and
whom Eden dislikes), he gently insists that he must deny himself even
the pleasure of helping his friends:

> 'Don't you see,' he said, 'that I can't do that? If I admit I have the
> power to dispose of it, why then I haven't got rid of the chains. I've
> got to let it slide: I mustn't allow myself the satisfaction of giving it to
> a friend' – and he looked at George – 'or selling it and giving the
> money to charity. I'm compelled to forgo even that. I must stand by
> as humbly as I can and be glad I haven't got the power.'[30]

It is greatly to Snow's credit that Martineau, instead of emerging as an
insufferable fool, should be such an engaging, subtle and likeable
character.[31] Of all the people in the books Martineau seems the least
weighed down by life. Without any of the theological jargon we are
made to feel that he has cast off his burden of care and walks lightened and
happy. Martineau appears to be the Christian ideal of humility, the
extreme opposite of Roy Calvert's spiritual pride, which stands in the way
of peace, for Roy tells Eliot:

> I've had the absolute conviction – it's much more real than anything
> one can see or touch – that God and his world exist. And everyone
> can enter and find their rest. Except me. I'm infinitely far away for
> ever. I am alone and apart and infinitesimally small – and I can't
> come near.[32]

But actually, the underlying ego is as strong as with Calvert; it merely takes a
less obvious form.

In the last group of characters considered in this chapter are Martin Eliot
in *The New Men* and Roger Quaife in *Corridors of Power*, who are placed in

situations where they are forced to make a choice which will radically alter the course of their lives. *The New Men* is about the making of the bomb and the struggles of conscience on the part of the scientists once it has been used. Martin Eliot, Lewis Eliot's younger brother, is a scientist working under Walter Luke at the Barford Atomic Establishment. Once it is known that the enemy is making a bomb there is no choice left but to make one themselves. The English, of course, never finally make it because the Americans do it first. But the English scientists are horrified when the bomb is dropped on Hiroshima. Martin writes a letter to *The Times* publicly denouncing it but Lewis Eliot dissuades him from sending it off. Ideals are all very well but Eliot, himself a responsible civil servant, knows that if Martin's letter is published it would mean the end of his career. For a brother as for a son, he says, one's concern is prosaic and crude. He has seen his friends throw away respectability, power and fame – Roy Calvert, Charles March, old Martineau – and he had understood why. Martin is different.

> But they were friends, and Martin was a brother. The last thing you want with a brother is that he should fulfil a poetic destiny.[33]

Lewis Eliot talks his brother out of it by saying that the letter will only be a pathetically defiant gesture; Martin could do more good from within when the time is ripe.

There is a choice to be made on the plane of ideas and Martin makes it too readily and perfunctorily. Does he really want to make his gesture or is he glad to be talked out of it? Lewis Eliot admits that his reasoning prevailed only because, deep within himself, Martin himself had fears about his idealistic gesture.

There is another confrontation between the brothers, much more deeply involved and complex, out of which Martin's final choice seems to me to really spring, although Snow blurs the issue at that point. There is at Barford a scientist called Sawbridge who is suspected of leaking information to Russia. Martin, a clever politician who knows that conservatism in such matters always pays, condemns Sawbridge and schemes for office at Luke's expense. Walter Luke, much more open and trusting than Martin but much less far-sighted, refuses to be suspicious of Sawbridge. This generous attitude is used by Martin to his own advantage. He joins in the hunt for Sawbridge, makes him break down and confess and duly impresses Whitehall with his administrative ability. Though he is much inferior as a scientist to Luke, the Government offers him the headship of Barford.

Through all this Lewis Eliot has been watching his brother in angry disapproval, knowing that he is scheming for position in an unworthy way. They exchange bitter words; when Lewis Eliot tells Martin that he has wanted a great deal for him, Martin replies angrily: 'No,' he said, 'You have wanted a good deal for yourself.'[34] When eventually the offer of the headship comes, Martin thinks it over and refuses it. There is, it appears to me, real confusion in the novelist's mind at this point in the novel. Martin refuses, surely, out of a sense of decency. Calculating and hard-headed as he is, he knows what is actually owed to Walter Luke and he steps down. All the events and conversation leading up to Martin's decision point to such an explanation for his behaviour. But Snow explains it differently. While the choice seems to me from textual evidence to arise out of a personal code of right behaviour, Martin is made by the author to justify it on entirely different grounds, going back to the Hiroshima letter state of mind. He tells his brother that he will go back to pure science and give up Barford because he does not want to be associated with destructive warfare:

> For any of us who had been concerned with the bomb, he repeated Luke's earlier comment, there was no clear-cut way out . . . there were just two conceivable ways. One was the way he had just taken: the other, to struggle on . . . and hope that we might come out at the end of the tunnel.[35]

This makes it sound as if he is giving up the position because, on principle, he wants to have nothing more to do with the bomb. But the reflections and intentions leading up to his renunciation clearly arise from the Sawbridge espionage case. Martin dislikes what he has done; he cannot in conscience accept the fruits of his scheming. His moral choice seems to me to be intimately connected with his political manoeuvrings but no mention of it is made at the end.

What makes the renunciation significant is that he is a born administrator and would have excelled at the job; he is *not* a first-class scientist. He goes back to a Fellowship at his old college knowing what a dim end this is for him, for he is not really meant for research. Like Arthur Miles in *The Search* Martin tries to reshape his life. The final chapter of *The New Men*, in which we see Martin living out daily the consequences of his renunciation, is a fine one. His confidence has gone, he is nervous in front of his bright young juniors, he has lost his high spirits; yet he is happy in a quiet way. There is a lightening of the weight of worldly care, a frail sort of cheer.

The earlier conflict over Hiroshima is not very significant to our understanding of Martin, for the simple reason that most of the scientists in the novel feel much the same way and Snow here is recording a group reaction rather than a personal dilemma. Rabinovitz claims that there is no moral choice at all in the book because the English never really made the bomb at that time in spite of the research expended on it, and concludes that Snow thus 'diminishes the possibility of any real moral choice about the use of the bomb'.[36] This is fair enough, but Rabinovitz ignores Martin's giving up of high office in which moral choice does seem to play an important part.

Martin Eliot is not an especially likeable character. He is far too taciturn, close-lipped and strained to be engaging. But the final picture of him in his college is a touching one. It is a strange end for a man with his skills; but he is a humbler and better man, sobered by life, quieter than ever. It is interesting to see that there was no natural situation to test Martin. He himself created a situation in the pursuit of his goal, then turned away from it out of a sense of honour.

Roger Quaife in *Corridors of Power* is a full-length study of the responsibility of the individual to live by his beliefs. A bright young Conservative minister just about the time of the Suez crisis, he upholds a disarmament policy for Britain as a first step towards dropping out of the arms race. His policy is based on economic, political and scientific grounds but beneath it all is plain human concern about nuclear war. This humanitarian angle is never stressed; the only explicit statement of Quaife's idealism is found in his final speech in Parliament in which he forgets all the temptations to safeguard himself by woolliness and obscurities, and says simply that Britain can do her bit for sanity even if she is no longer a superpower:

> ... I am certain that we can help – by example, by good judgement, by talking sense, and acting sense – we can help swing the balance between a good future and a bad future, or between a good future and none at all. We can't contract out.[37]

This is what he has believed in all along and he comes out with it at the end.

Snow has succeeded admirably in creating a sense of the complexities and uncertainties that hedge true motive and the near impossibility of making simple choices. If one is to do good one must have power; to get that power one must compromise. Quaife becomes a minister by cleverly manoeuvring Gilbey out of that position,[38] but having attained the office, he is able to act with greater vision than Gilbey. Eliot, who considers Roger Quaife a deeply forested character, even wonders when he finds a colleague, Cave, attacking him at a dinner-party, whether the whole scene has not been stage-managed to show him up to advantage. He comments:

> It had been convenient for Roger, it had suited his tactics, for the attack to be made.[39]

Even while he cautiously tries out his disarmament policy, he is wary of unpopularity and leaves himself a line of retreat:

> Of course he must have faced the thought ... that there was still time to back down, throw the stress of his policy just where solid men would be comfortable, then take another Ministry, and gain considerable credit into the bargain.[40]

There is a real moment of temptation for Quaife to withdraw from his policy when David Rubin, the famous American scientist who had earlier told him that England did not count in the arms race, now tells him that it is still important for England to stay in it and not appear to be swimming against the tide by pushing the disarmament policy. According to Rubin, America is worried that her allies might slide out of the Cold War and knows that the West badly needs all the moral support it can get. Rubin feels that the climate is such that, if Quaife presses his policy when his country is not ready for it, his political career will be finished. He advises him to drift along for the moment; perhaps ten years later the time will be right. Rubin asks:

> Does one person matter very much? Can any one person do very much?[41]

Roger Quaife, who is grateful for Rubin's concern for his political career, cannot go along with this advice because he feels there are occasions when morality grows out of action and this is one of them. Not to carry out his disarmament policy now would be a betrayal of his ideals. He replies:

> In that case, one might as well not be here at all. Anyone could just wait until it's easy. I don't think I should have lived this life if that were all.[42]

He pursues his policy, is defeated by a far larger number of votes than expected and walks out of the House to the chant of 'Resign, resign'. The courage and rightness of Roger Quaife, the humanity and compassion underlying his policy, the fact that liberal scientists and men of sense all agree about what he stands for – these facts are never overplayed. The animosity he runs into, the difficulty of urging any truly radical measure through the parliamentary procedure, these are well evoked. It is largely through this that Quaife's idealism is suggested. If he can continue to believe what he does in the thick of this unwelcoming climate, obviously he is an idealist. The moral choice is between action and non-action. Not to do right would be as immoral as doing wrong.

This chapter has considered the ways in which many of Snow's characters find out what they live for or, having found it, live by their beliefs as best they can. Their circumstances are widely different – the poor boy from the provinces, the scholar in the college, the rich Jew, the scientist during the war, the politician in Parliament – each of these either resolves his problem or succumbs. Resolution is usually in terms of an outward social concern. Whether it is Lewis Eliot, Martin Eliot, Charles March or Roger Quaife, consideration for other people or interest in society is an essential part of their humanity. Their actions seldom bring much cheerfulness at the end but they do bring a serenity of sorts, a satisfaction at having behaved with reasonable unselfishness.

One might say with Matthew Arnold that 'calm's not life's crown though calm is well', but given the complications of the modern context and the tone of the modern mood, ecstasy is not very appropriate. Heroism and the tragic stance seem extravagant to the contemporary reader. Given that mood, these modest moral aims seem sufficiently demanding. To achieve even these, loyalty, compassion, tolerance and unselfishness, Snow suggests, is difficult enough.

This set of values may sound old-fashioned, which is perhaps the reason why Snow has been regarded in some quarters as one of the most deeply backward-looking and nostalgic of novelists. Kingsley Amis, when interviewed not very long ago by Melvyn Bragg in *The Listener*, said about one of his own novels that he considered it as an elegy for 'the passing of that great set of certainties – all those values to do with chastity, loyalty, conventionality, behaving as you should behave, not getting above yourself, patience, being ready to accept experience but in a selective way, not accepting everything and viewing everything you see with a careful critical eye, above all, of course, having powerful but very vague ideas of right and wrong'.[43] Reading that, it struck me as a good description of Snow's own preoccupations. His own 'set of certainties' is very close to what Amis has set down there.

For what is a man profited if he shall gain the whole world and lose his own soul? This is the question that lies unobtrusively behind Snow's novels, unobtrusive because the values of the spirit are not won by his characters through outright rejection of the world.

I hope that this examination of the lives of Snow's characters shows that worldly success is not all-important in his fictional world. On the other hand, Snow does not believe, as was said in the *TLS* in a different context, that 'the successful world is a stuffy one and only the reasonably unambitious ones are congenial companions'.[44] However, because Snow does not emphasise the religious temperament and makes no obvious sharp distinction between the ideal and the pragmatic, he has been at times criticised for not showing the worldly life as sufficiently harmful to the spirit and for being too much impressed by honours and success. Melancholy as he is about the isolation of the individual, he believes on the whole that through reason and a civilised rational will, man can and should live meaningfully in this world, for this life is the only one we have. The usual consolations of religion are not acceptable to him and there is nothing beyond this existence. Therefore men must live this life in this world or not at all. Hence the importance of success but the greater importance of self-knowledge and honesty. Both the attractions of office and the hold of idealism are present to the heroes of Snow's fiction, and the nearest he comes to hinting at an ideal type is through the man of action in touch with his own experience. Action by itself, and you have a crass and bouncing Swaffield; introspection alone, and you have a hopeless Calvert. The ideal is to achieve a harmony between action and introspection, seen to some extent in the person of Lewis Eliot.

But perhaps it would be truer to say that there is no fully realised ideal type at all in the world of his novels. There is too strong a sense of human failing and inadequacy for Snow to exult or rejoice over anything, and given that bleak and spare cast of mind, no one heroic type can be vividly projected. Not that there is much agony or despair, but there is a definite absence of joy. We seem to move in an in-between region of the spirit where man may partially redeem himself through self-knowledge and humility.

4 Groups and enclaves

A recurring theme in Snow's novels is that of 'man in conference', a subject which no other novelist has handled with the same sustained curiosity and sense of conviction. In dealing with the inner workings of groups and the confrontation of individuals with groups, Snow demonstrates a sensitive aliveness not only to the language and matter but also to the many psychological undercurrents that surface on such occasions. The clearest treatment of groups and the men who comprise them are to be found in his novels *The Masters* and *The Affair* but more isolated examples can also be found in *The Search* and *Homecomings*. Illustrations in this chapter of Snow's thoughts on what constitutes a group and holds it together, and on the individuals both snugly within it and loftily outside it, will be taken mainly from the four novels mentioned above.

In these novels Snow unfolds what Mandel has called 'the drama of management',[1] cleverly orchestrating the various elements at play when men are gathered together in the conference room. Whether it is a meeting of the Fellows at a Cambridge college, of civil servants in Whitehall, of scientists during the war, or Ministers and Members of Parliament, we hear the seldom-raised voices of the committee members, judiciously compromising even when partisan feelings run high, protecting sensitive egos and straining to maintain a rational appearance at all costs. Once in a while, when someone breaks out of the carefully handled situation (as Roy Calvert does at a meeting to celebrate the seventieth birthday of a distinguished Orientalist, or as Lewis Eliot does when George Passant is not made permanent in the Civil Service), tensions can build up and the sparks fly. Otherwise the sensible phrases soothe and cajole ruffled feelings, the smoothly-balanced 'orotundities' roll on and the imperturbable surface is wonderfully maintained! It is typical of Snow's conference men that they seldom let themselves verbally 'rip', however irrational the springs of their action. Despard-Smith in *The Masters,* for instance, an embittered old clergyman with the smell of whisky on his breath, explains to Lewis Eliot that he will not vote for Jago because he is himself a disappointed man and would like to see another's longing likewise disappointed.[2] The undertones are full of rancour but no storm is let loose; there is no flooding of emotion; the panoply of reasonable conversation is kept up.

Snow's groups are exclusively privileged or elitist and usually composed of educated professional men. In an article in the *TLS* entitled 'In the Communities of the Elite'[3] Snow gives two possible reasons for writing about such coteries. First, he sees them, whether academic, administrative, political or whatever, as little enclaves of order in society which is otherwise multifarious and disorderly. Exploration of such limited groups which are bound by certain common interests might make, in Snow's opinion, for increased lucidity and they are therefore rewarding as subjects in fiction. In a world of 'maximum mixed-up-ness' only such groups can possibly take the place of the limited sections of society which, for the sake of compactness and elegance, Jane Austen and Anthony Trollope had dealt with in their novels at an earlier time. Secondly, Snow says that members of an elite are 'freer in personality', richer in contrasts and psychologically more exciting to a writer and that the dilemmas and ethical situations a writer needs are ready at hand.[2]

It may be argued that by isolating the segments of society he fictionalises, Snow has, like Jane Austen, achieved comprehensibility at the expense of comprehensiveness. In Jane Austen's novels, as has often been remarked, we hear nothing about the Napoleonic Wars but we seem to know every house and street in Highbury. In the same way, in Snow's *The Masters* we hear the ringing tones of old Professor Gay and the comfortable chuckles of Arthur Brown but the outside world verging on the Second World War comes in only peripherally, if at all, as when Pillbrow changes his vote in the election for the Master because of the political situation.

The groups in Snow's novels are held together by tradition and ritual. To feel part of a continuing tradition gives a soothing sense of security to the members of the group. These are places of retreat and, however troubled in spirit the men may be who participate in the meetings, they are drawn together, they are clubbable and they can obtain a temporary sense of reassurance from the unflurried voices and the comforting outward forms to which they have agreed to conform. 'Flummery' is Snow's amused but affectionate word for ritual. He enjoys it all immensely, down to the entering of a name in the wine-book to record the presentation of a celebratory bottle of wine in a college common-room. Clergymen have done this since the seventeenth century and Snow hopes that it will go on thus; this is part of an 'Englishness' which has its value. In *Last Things* Lewis Eliot observes:

It had perhaps been a strength sometimes, this national passion for clinging on to forms, nostalgic, pious, wart-hog obstinate.[5]

Snow suggests that the ritual ceremonies and after-dinner conversations and the forms of an institution can contain and calm down dangerous drives. Sharp voices get muffled and security settles over the members of the group rather like a blanket.

Snow's exclusive society exudes a cosiness, practically a visceral warmth. One gets the feeling that the windows are shut and all bolts drawn against the bitter winds outside.[6] The customary setting in his academic novels is a blazing fire in a curtained room with walnuts and wine after dinner. The rich country houses where politicians spend weekends, Sir Hector Rose's office, bowl of chrysanthemums and all, where civil servants gather for a meeting – all exude this same sense of security.[7] In *Last Things* Snow describes the guest room in the House of Lords thus:

> ... as we sat in a window-seat looking over the river, lights on the south bank aureoled in the November mist, people greeted him with the kind of euphoria that one met in other kinds of enclave such as a college or a club.[8]

Richard Mayne refers to this assured sense of solidity when he says that opening a Snow novel is a 'little like sinking into a comfortable armchair' and that there is 'an atmosphere of mahogany and waistcoats that's familiar in a curious way'.[9] Significantly, in the later novels, anxiety increasingly invades the warmth and security of such enclaves. It is not possible to exclude illness and death. Snow's latest novel, *In Their Wisdom,* is set in one of the grandest of such cosy societies, the House of Lords, hung in crimson and gold, but still pervaded by the deepest sort of anxieties.

Snow is chiefly preoccupied in showing how groups act and arrive at the decisions so important to the running of the machinery of modern life. He has repeatedly delineated the complex and subtle relationship between the individual and the group. His insistent advice to any individual interested in the decision of a committee is: never be too proud to be present in the flesh. An absent person in a committee counts for nothing at all and the loyalty and sentiment of friends can do little for him by proxy. Snow is here emphasising the fact that conflicts of opinion are inevitably resolved in committees by a match of wills and, if one is not present to match one's own against the wills of others, one can hardly expect a resolution in one's favour. He also emphasises the ability to compromise as an important attribute for the individual's effectiveness within the group.

Snow draws an interesting opposition between the ordinary but successful group man and the extraordinary, finer-fibred individual who cannot be easily drawn into a group. Snow suggests that the effective committee man is not likely to be the most brilliant man but rather the one who has the most staying-power with a clear and intelligent grasp of the situation. The most successful illustration of these virtues is Arthur Brown, who is tutor at the Cambridge college of which Lewis Eliot is a Fellow. Practised and smooth, he can steer the obvious course with skill and keep tempers on an even keel. However, he has no spark of originality, nor any special insight, and in real life is probably dull, uninspired and unexciting. Yet the novelist has made him an extremely likeable person whom we enjoy hearing and reading about. He has his own sort of understanding; when his close friend, Chrystal, wrecks the electoral campaign he has so carefully handled, he is calmly resigned to the situation. He accepts men as they are, treacherous one moment, loyal the next:

> One took them as they were. That gave Brown his unfailing strength, and also a tinge, deep under the comfortable flesh, of ironic sadness.[10]

Another example of a good committee man is Houston Eggar, at first dismissed as somewhat dim but of whom Eliot later notes:

> . . . he was surprisingly effective in committee; he was not particularly clever, but he spoke with clarity, enthusiasm, pertinacity and above all weight. Even among sophisticated men, weight counted immeasurably more than subtlety or finesse.[11]

The group does not readily tolerate extreme individuality. In turn, Jago, Howard and Passant have to be excluded if the group equilibrium is to be maintained. Too much of anything – emotion (Jago), radicalism (Howard) or anarchism (Passant) – is inevitably expelled. Mandel has characterised this method of stabilising society from which the guilty 'other' is removed, as a 'scapegoat solution'.[12] In many cases the disturbing men are more brilliant (Passant) or magnetic (Jago) than those around them, but groups prefer the sound and the second-rate to the more flamboyant and flashy personalities. The Master, who has had a lot of trouble before he manages to get Roy Calvert elected as a Fellow, remarks to his brother-in-law: 'No society of men is very fond of brilliance, Hugh.'[13]

Are we to conclude from the facts that Jago loses the election, that Passant is not made permanent in Whitehall and that Howard's Fellowship is allowed to expire, that Snow himself approves of middling mediocrity and tends to regard the outstanding with suspicion and dislike? Far from it. Eliot, Snow's *alter ego,* is strongly committed to all these three men; he fights for them as much as he can. In *Homecomings,* after George Passant has been interviewed, he clashes bitterly with Sir Hector Rose who refused to run the risk of taking on a man of 'powerful and perhaps faintly unstable personality'. Lewis Eliot loses his temper.

> I said they were too fond of the second-rate. I said that any society which deliberately made safe appointments was on the way out.[14]

Wretched because he cannot help George Passant, who is more brainy than the rest of them put together but also more singular in personality, Eliot reflects:

> The men I sat with in their offices, with their comfortable, conforming indignation which never made them put a foot out of step – they were the men who managed the world, they were the people who in society came out on top. They had virtues denied the rest of us: I had to give them my respect. But that morning I was on the other side.[15]

Lewis Eliot, as is evident from the quotation above, combines the elements of both: the balance and control of the effective group-man and the bolder and freer imagination of the exceptional individual. He is unquestionably intelligent and imaginative, but with his acquired discretion and control he can sit on committees with usefulness and even interest. He recognises that the group makes for stability although often at the expense of excluding the extraordinary and the fine. On the whole, the comforting pull of an institution is something that he feels is moderately valuable; it exercises a set of checks and balances and makes fanaticism less likely. If Lewis Eliot has to be classified either as an outsider-individual or as one of the group-men, he would have to be placed, somewhat uncomfortably, within the group. He belongs there by temperament more naturally than Passant or Calvert or Charles March. At the same time, he is obviously more imaginative than, say, Arthur Brown or Hector Rose.

At the other extreme, people like Roy Calvert and Eustace Pillbrow are quite unsuccessful as group-men. Roy Calvert, who is subtle and perceptive when alone with any man, is strangely maladroit when confronted with a group of men. Eliot notes that Roy never got the ear of a college meeting. Eustace Pillbrow, distinguished scholar and youthfully gay despite his seventy years, is another person unable to project himself into a committee. Both he and Roy Calvert are too natural; they cannot maintain proper decorum as the platitudes are being sounded and the 'old familiar phrases sent reverberating around'. They are too much above the battle, not ordinary enough. So, though both have international reputations for their scholarship, nothing can make them effective at college meetings. Eliot comments:

> Pillbrow did much good, Roy Calvert was often selfless; but neither of them was humble enough to learn the language of more ordinary men.[16]

Out of the opposition presented by Snow between the extraordinary individual and the mediocre but effective group-man an interesting question arises: are the Arthur Browns being held up to us as the ideal managers? Are the Arthur Browns and the Hector Roses the heroes that the twentieth century has to offer? Certainly they are presented straight; there is no mockery, no touch of irony in the novelist's attitude towards them. If so, what has happened to imagination? Should not our reaction be, as Winslow's is when Brown's name is proposed as an alternative candidate:

'My dear Dean', said Winslow, 'it would mean twenty years of stodge.'[17]

Are these worthy but dull men to be the leaders of our society?

I believe the answer is: there could be worse. These men are at least fair and deliberate; they promise a certain amount of safety and security from violence and cruelty. They are honest and fair; that by itself should count for something in a world that has survived Auschwitz. Crawford's remark in *The Affair* about sensible men usually reaching sensible conclusions is a bitter irony, but on the whole the groups do seem to move in the direction of fair action. The extraordinary individual by contrast becomes a potential source of danger; he is capable of being swept along the tide of his own emotion or belief to a point where he may become a threat to society. Roy Calvert, in his search for authority is, for instance, attracted by the Nazi power in Germany; George Passant, on the other hand, is a confirmed radical. The point is that neither of them can maintain a balance in whatever they do and, dear as they are to Eliot, are seen in the end as corrupting influences.

Snow's resolution of the conflict between the individual and the group seems to be that the individual as a person and as a non-political creature is of intrinsic interest and value and that his private conflicts and tensions are to be regarded with tolerance, sympathy and understanding. In fact, human weakness, having to know and forgive oneself, is central to Snow's idea of the matured human being. But in public life he does not completely place his trust on any single individual, however fine-fibred and idealistic he might be.

In the process of exposing the workings of groups and the hidden factors influencing group decisions, Snow catches with astonishing realism the drama of the committee-room. Nothing goes as plainly and smoothly as one would expect from a gathering of rational and educated men. Pet aversions, cherished grudges, minor snubs and rankling disappointments, all disguised under the veneer of politeness and beautifully articulated sentences, are shown to exert their subtle roles in the making of group decisions. An excellent example of egos that jostle one another is to be found in Snow's first serious novel, *The Search*. A committee of hardened academics from the leading universities meet to plan the setting up of an Institute of Biophysics. Snow does not usually resort to satire but here, his deadpan, detached manner as he describes the different men pulling in different directions, each concerned in his distinctive way about his own convenience and importance, is very effective. The alacrity with which they let themselves be sidetracked from the important issue, to discuss for hours the question of buildings; the several sessions that they fritter away before they can decide even on the venue of the committee's meetings – all of this is rendered with a sharpness of tone not elsewhere to be found in Snow. The personalities of the men come across from the way they sit in their chairs and the way they form their sentences. Notice, for instance, Fane, the professor from Manchester, half-turned in his chair, half speaking over his shoulder, a smile on his 'subtle ecclesiastical' face, inwardly eaten up by jealousy and contempt and scornfully making literary allusions which Desmond pretends to understand; or Desmond himself, the salesman of science from Oxford, roguish and wavering; or Austin from London, portly, pontifical, paunched, 'leaning back and breathing hard'; or Constantine, wild and eloquent, ill at ease; or Pritt from Cambridge, eyes opaque and dull. The subtlety of shades that Snow has caught in the portraits of these men is astonishing. Once they have decided the meeting-place of the committee, they quarrel bitterly over where the institute is to be located. Austin wants it for London, 'simply, sturdily and all the time'; Desmond wants it for Oxford ('The old colleges want this kind of thing. It would brace the colleges up. It would make them zip.'); Pritt wants it for Cambridge, for himself; Fane will have it anywhere as long as Constantine is nowhere near it – he resents any ability greater than his own. Such is Snow's early picture of distinguished scientists; he is less sharp-edged and more respectful in the later novels.

Another fine illustration of Snow's handling of committee decisions is found in the second interview of George Passant for a permanent place in the Civil Service. Besides Lewis Eliot there are three other members on the panel of whom Sir Hector Rose is the most senior and the one with whom the decision really rests. He is highly efficient, has a trained professional mind and extravagantly courteous manners, but is steely within. He is also, within human limits, fair. But he dislikes George and from the first has opposed his coming in even on a temporary appointment. They are extreme contrasts. Hector Rose is a man in pefect control of himself with a blankly youthful appearance and exquisitely bland manners; George shows signs of strain and looks like one who has found his temperament difficult to manage. Eliot reflects when George is first being interviewed:

> His shoes, his tie, separated him from Rose as much as his accent did, and there was not only class, there was success dividing them.[18]

The second member of the panel, John Jones, has made a lifetime's occupation of pleasing and surviving and is now just a year away from retirement. At each point he waits to see which way Rose inclines and chimes in, managing just enough difference of opinion as to make him sound genuine. He has it all carefully planned and he is, says Eliot, hypnotised by his own technique. He knows that his opinion does not really count beside that of Osbaldistone, twenty-five years his junior.

The third member, Douglas Osbaldistone, is a rising Treasury official, and it is rumoured of him that he will get to the very top, further even than Hector Rose. Socially he has come a long way, from lower down in society than even Lewis Eliot. The thumbnail sketch tells us a good deal:

> ... born in the East End, a scholarship, Oxford, the Civil Service examination. In the Treasury he had fitted so precisely that it seemed, though it was not, a feat of impersonation: Christian names, the absence of jargon, the touch of insouciant cultivation carried like a volume in the pocket – they all sounded like his native speech.[19]

Eliot's account of George's performance before the members of the interviewing panel is exact, with the anxiety of someone personally involved: he records George's fantastic record of fact but decides it was a shade too buoyant. In the end Osbaldistone is impressed but not enough to oppose strenuously Hector Rose's meticulously phrased reasons for not having him. Given George's singularity he would be a mild risk; conceivably there might even be some commotion or row that might be set off by his personality. Osbaldistone does not care to oppose Rose in his judgement. Jones's contribution after Hector Rose's opinion is:

> 'Well,' said Jones, 'I don't think anyone could add much to a summing up like that.'[20]

The meeting is a fine display of personalities modified by the conference. Most dominating of all is Hector Rose. His judgement may be rooted in dislike but, given his Civil Service moorings, it is superbly rationalised. Compared to him Jones is the complete nonentity, beautifully realised by an anxious question here, a concurrence there. Osbaldistone, fair, unbiased and uncommitted, is impressive in his own right; he is perhaps the one whose opinion is most to be relied on. In contrast, Eliot appears as fiercely partisan, angry with them all. And there is George Passant himself, awkward and a misfit in this company of what may be described, to use a phrase coined by R. A. Butler about the Civil Service, as 'silky minds'.

In the clash of wills between Rose and Eliot, Rose emerges as the winner with his temper kept in cold control, an asset which Snow clearly recognises as important in a successful committee-man.

I should like now to consider an incident in which Snow shows how the individual modifies his own behaviour when confronted by the group, whether in a desire to please, impress or appease. In the novel *The Masters*, Jago, a candidate for the mastership, has a bitter antagonist called Winslow for whom he has little regard. Yet, in a confrontation between Winslow and Chrystal (one of Jago's supporters), Jago puts up a piece of bravura supporting his old enemy and by implication belittling his friend. Why does Jago do it? He defends Winslow perhaps because he finds that a flamboyant gesture in public can bring him a secret glow of heroism. But it is as warm a gesture as it is an egotistical one. Though it is hard to imagine Jago supporting Winslow in solitude, his performance in public is not totally a piece of insincerity; he is shown to be overcome by the emotion of the moment and feels momentarily Winslow's bitter sense of outrage. He senses that Winslow needs sympathy; he is quick to feel it stirring within himself; he sees others watching and he simply cannot resist making the gesture at that moment. While there is a spark of genuine sympathy it seems to be fanned into a glow by the occasion, the fact of being watched by others; the audience releases a latent histrionic streak and he makes an exaggerated response.

In the same novel, Chrystal is shown as venting his desire to influence the action of the group in a decisive way when he switches his vote for the mastership from Jago to Crawford, and by giving Crawford the desired majority to end the stalemate, gains temporary control of events around him. Chrystal's gradual change of heart and mind about Jago is brilliantly traced and comes about naturally and inevitably. He is driven by personal considerations of self, but hurt vanity also plays its part because Jago does not, in his flaring momentary sympathy for Winslow, show proper appreciation of the enormous donation Chrystal has secured for the college. As Brown's great friend, Chrystal had supported his candidate Jago with his usual vigour at the start but, since the control of the campaign is in Brown's hands, he busies himself with getting a huge benefaction for the college from a rich industrialist. When he is finally able to announce that he has secured it and Winslow, the Bursar, resigns in protest for not having been consulted earlier, crystal watches Jago's gesture of support for Winslow with undisguised chagrin. Gradually he slides away from his friend Brown's 'steady, imperceptible guidance' and wrecks Jago's chances by withdrawing his support at the crucial vote. This is not merely simple revenge; all kinds of factors have been slowly suggested: Chrystal's unthinking and impetuous consent to support Jago; his subconscious desire to free himself of Brown's influence; the satisfaction at his nerve-ends when he is busy in with the rich industrialist; the flattered ego that can announce an important benefaction; his discovery that the emotional Jago is not a person with whom he is temperamentally much in sympathy, a question he had not asked himself before; and of course, hurt vanity. Eliot reflects on Chrystal's feeling about the magisterial election:

He had never been master of the events round him. It was that which he could not forgive.[21]

And a little later:

Envy and pique and vanity, all the passions of self-regard; you could not live long in a society of men and not see them often weigh down the rest. How much of my own objection to Crawford was because he once spoke of me as a barrister manqué?[22]

Let us now turn our attention to the most striking characteristics of the nature of groups: inertia, lethargy and an innate unwillingness to be unduly disturbed. This is abundantly manifest in *The Affair* where we see how an institution, in this case the Cambridge college of *The Masters,* grumblingly goes into action to accomplish fairness and justice. Donald Howard, a Fellow, has been deprived of his fellowship on suspicion of scientific fraud. New evidence later casts doubt on that judgement. While there are a few people like Skeffington and Lewis and Martin Eliot to take the initiative and fight for justice for the wronged man, most of the other members of the group are content to remain passive because they are irritated by the demands on their time that any action would make. However, all sense of justice is not totally lost and, with a strong enough case, Skeffington succeeds in getting a reinvestigation started. The initial apathy of the other Fellows does not belie the fact that, when all is said and done, the English are still believers in fair play, the sporting spirit, and all the other virtues learned on the Eton playing-fields. What makes all this old hat interesting is: first, the conservatism and prejudice of the academics; and second, the degree to which they are swayed by personal mana. Donald Howard's political opinions are red; therefore he is a man not to be trusted at any point on any matter. On the other hand, if Sir Francis Getliffe, established scientist, comes out in favour of Howard, it can shake many of the rigid old men. What is good enough for Francis Getliffe is good enough for Winslow. It is surprising that justice gets done at all given these prejudices. The fact that they are willing to carry on with Nightingale as Bursar, even though Getliffe's evidence points to his having removed the crucial photograph which would have cleared Howard beyond all doubt, shows how content they are that things should go on as they have always been. As a group they do not demand Nightingale's resignation; that would mean more disturbance. Many of them are old men and they would like to be left in peace.

What we have said so far concerns Snow's version of 'closed politics', the small group where personal considerations and strong wills tend to carry the day. About larger bureaucracies he says nothing so definite. He makes, in fact, a sort of mystique about power and the formulation of decision. Cutting down the commonly-held notion that important and powerful men make their own decisions and shape the course of history, Snow apparently feels that no single person in office, especially political office, makes very much difference. No one really knows where the power lies; the final policy that emerges may crystallise out of a hundred small decisions and crossed-out statements. Snow would dismiss as 'romantic' the notion that governmental policy is boldly conceived or clearly formulated by great leaders. The administrators or civil servants who remain faceless and unknown have a lot more to do with the shaping of official policy than is generally believed; power vanishes under the heaps of files lying on the desks of the secretaries and under-secretaries. Eliot observes:

> ... one saw policy shaped under one's eyes by a series of small decisions .... Usually it built itself from a thousand small arrangements, ideas, compromises, bits of give and take.[23]

Snow emphasises the benevolence of power which emanates from such diffuse sources. Lewis Eliot, his chief character, is happy about power and decisions coming from a group like this rather than from 'great leaders'. He says to a Nazi official just before the war:

> No one is fit to be trusted with power. No one .... Any man who has lived at all knows the follies and wickedness he's capable of. If he does not know it, he is not fit to govern others. And if he does know it, he knows also that neither he nor any man ought to be allowed to decide a single human fate.[24]

This passage is especially interesting because it sees safety in numbers. Self-knowledge, knowing the corruption one is oneself capable of, makes one wary of absolute power in anyone else. In another novel, *The Conscience of the Rich,* Eliot is made to explain much the same thing to Ann Simon, a Communist friend who is inviting him to join the party:

> Any regime of her kind just had to give its bosses great power without any check. Granted that they were aiming at good things, it was still too dangerous. People with power began to get detached from anything but power itself. No one could be trusted with power for long.[25]

The fact that Eliot is a liberal, well left of centre in his political faith, does not make him more sympathetic to communism than to Nazi fascism because he basically distrusts concentration of power under any political guise. A group which 'muddles through' as in *The Affair* is much more to be trusted than any charismatic leader. Snow's unvarnished picture of the irrational in-fighting and bickerings that go on inside committee rooms and his fascinated analysis of the myriad motives that govern group decisions leave us little or nothing to cheer about, but at least, he seems to say, they are less to be feared because they pull in different directions.

In his delineation of big groups and bureaucratic organisations,

Snow, as a novelist, is breaking new ground. He makes us aware of how people today get a large sense of identity from their jobs, much more, say, than in the eighteenth century when the novels of the time would have us believe that such identity was to be gained through roadside adventures or sexual escapades. The emphasis shifted somewhat in the nineteenth-century English novel where, after the Industrial Revolution, what one 'did' for a living gradually became a matter of pride and not a subject of concealment. For the first time, business houses, lawyers' offices and doctors' rooms begin to appear as natural backdrops for the actions of men. But it is only in present-day society that the wheels within wheels have become so clearly and rigidly defined, and the ups and downs of the professional life which contribute so much to the stress and pressure of modern-day existence have become proper subjects for detailed treatment. The identity of many of Snow's characters comes largely from what they do. Francis Getliffe, the clever and high-minded scientist, is identified essentially by the work he does; so too Hector Rose, the civil servant; Herbert Getliffe, the clever lawyer; Walter Luke, the Government scientist; and Nightingale the chemist, later Bursar of the college. What they do is their *raison d'être*.

In the re-creation of such themes as we have discussed in this chapter – groups both big and small; their nature and the way they work; the relationship of the group and the individual; the formulation of group decisions and the importance of jobs in a bureaucratic society – Snow is undisputedly a master. He speaks with authority and conviction, doubtless because he has himself held office in several different fields. The *TLS* remarked in 1960 that most English novelists are educated in a way that precludes any wide range of practical experience and that many of them never do a day's work (in the actual sense) in their lives.[26] C. P. Snow has certainly entered that workaday world himself, and more, has fictionalised it with subtlety and knowledgeableness. Alan Pryce-Jones once plaintively wondered in the *TLS* why certain huge permanent themes are mildewed from neglect:

> It has always seemed to me a little strange that among a people like our own . . . so little has been done to explain what is going on above a certain level. Heads of state meet – or do not meet – governments rise and fall, bishops plunge into bright alternation of controversy and garden-party, young men are angry and old men forget, but the point of all these processes hardly gets discussed except briefly in the air or abruptly in a newspaper leader.[27]

That comment was made in 1958 and Alan Pryce-Jones perhaps did not specifically have novel-writing in mind, but Snow in many of his later novels has set out to fictionalise 'what is going on above a certain level'. If we compare him with Trollope, Disraeli, H. G. Wells and Galsworthy, all of whom have dealt with similar themes, it must be admitted that in this treatment of men at work in groups Snow is wider in range and has surpassed these earlier authors in skill. What a certain type of critic might bring against Snow is that he does not satirise the public life or the weakness of men when gathered together. The traditional approach of novelists and poets has been to show up the academics and politicians as complacent and absurdly deluded. But Snow takes these men seriously; nor is he unduly haunted by any world of nightmare that such men are likely to bring.

In his treatment of groups Snow is generally unjudging and understanding of all types of men and all manners of response. The tone of the narrator in his youthful novel *The Search* has an ironic edge and sharpness that we do not hear again till we come to his latest novels, *Last Things* and *In Their Wisdom*, where his patient tolerance of groups shows signs of wear. It is as if youth and old age have some common ground: in youth one has not quite learned patience; in old age one has got slightly tired of it all.

5 The darkening vision

While Snow in his novels has never at any time been caught up in a rap-
ture, he started out with a measure of hopefulness, as shown by the title
of an early volume, *Time of Hope*. But the phrase itself, evocative of
Ecclesiastes, carries the implication of transitoriness and hints that hope
was only for that place and that time. The novel unfolds the events and
experience that time brought in its train, taking away the hopefulness of
youth. Snow has so often been called a meliorist that one might usefully
recognise that, from the beginning, there is present in his fiction a strain
of bleakness and a real sense of human limitations. He has explicitly
said, both in the controversial Two Cultures lecture and in connection
with Martin Eliot in *The New Men,* that the individual life is tragic, that
each of us is alone and it is but a short way to the grave. Much more
significant than these statements is the continued awareness in the novels
of the buried tide of emotion, the tragic possibility, which flows beneath
all effort and action. What he does *not* afford in his novels is the cathartic
release of the tragic emotions: that is, while he recognises the tragic
stance, he never assumes it himself as a writer.

Underlying the later novels, and growing gradually with each
succeeding work, is a deepening pessimism. I believe that the explicit
expression of that begins with the publication of *Corridors of Power*. Till
then, Snow had suggested, in his quiet way, the upward and outward
movement, the rise to the seats of power; working out towards society,
doing the little good one can in terms of action. Exercising the will and
reason for moral ends seemed worth doing. Science promised great
things and the hope for society seemed to permeate the personal life as
well. Freedom from poverty and disease and the personal freedom to
live according to one's lights – these were exciting goals.

The time of hope Snow takes us back to was indeed a period of confidence and excitement for Britain. Empire was in its heyday at the dawn
of the century and the early twenties and thirties were years of tremen-

dous achievement for English science. The spirit of the time is best evoked by recalling the exuberant shade of the leading Cambridge physicist of the time, Lord Rutherford. When someone remarked to him that he seemed to be always riding on the crest of a wave, he is said to have replied: 'Well, I made the wave, didn't I?' Such was the feeling of self-confidence shared by scientists in general in England and elsewhere. It could almost be believed that there was no limit to human achievement; that almost all nature's secrets could be unravelled and surely would be. It certainly was the right dawn for a young scientist to be young and alive in, as Snow was. It is hardly surprising that he, in the thick of the excitement, while too temperately austere to evoke joy, felt about human life that it could be controlled and about human nature that it could be understood.

Closely related to the scientific confidence was the growth of the liberal ideal. Nineteenth-century science had succeeded so spectacularly in improving the quality of material life for the masses that the lower classes, now better fed and clothed and exposed to ideas of freedom and self-improvement, stirred with aspirations hitherto undreamed of. If poverty can be banished, all men will be left free to pursue their own causes in dignity and peace; they will begin to recognise the validity of different opinions. A technological and political millenium seemed at hand. The euphoria of the inter-war period ran high and who was to know that in a span of twenty years Britain would emerge exhausted, dazed and spent, slowly losing ground in a political and scientific climate that was changing the world at a stunning rate?

Snow's youthful hopefulness may be judged from William Cooper's *Scenes from Provincial Life,* where one of Cooper's characters, a civil servant named Robert, seems to me to be based on Snow, and indeed Snow, in a letter to me, has confirmed that this is so. From this portrait we can see that, as a young man, Snow must have had his share of gleeful fun.

Though there is no dramatic change in Snow's attitude, there is, starting from the late fifties, a very slow abandonment of his faith. That is why I have called this chapter 'The Darkening Vision'. The writer describes in *The Sleep of Reason* and *Last Things* how Eliot was operated on for detached retina of one eye, and Snow has confirmed that he himself has only peripheral vision now in that eye. It is not Snow's way to be symbolic to be sure, but that blurring of his actual vision seems to me to be accompanied by a blurring over of his spiritual certainties. The truths and objects he saw so clearly appear now to take on dim and threatening shapes. In a reversal here of St Paul's famous words, Eliot began by seeing things, as he imagined, clearly. But now, with illness plaguing both society and his own body, he sees through a glass darkly. Reasonable action, moral action, seems as far and dim and as obscured by patches and shadows as are the morning light and window-frame when he wakes up one morning and finds that his retina has got detached. With the loss of vision goes a loss of confidence about human nature and life itself; for the first time Lewis Eliot is up against experiences from which there is no appeal to reason. For a man whose life has rested on reason this is serious indeed, and it is hardly surprising that the meliorist in Snow goes underground and the pessimist surfaces.

What makes the movement from spring to winter so moving and real is the ageing of Lewis Eliot. It is entirely appropriate that old age should bring diminishing confidence and a slow withdrawal from society. But the fact that society has supplied very genuine reasons for loss of hope, while deplorable in itself, combines with the other personal darkening to make for an authentic and aesthetically satisfying development of Snow's fiction. Nor does he finally stop there. After the trials and glooms of the last two volumes of the *Strangers and Brothers* sequence, the writer recovers his balance with an appropriate detachment in his latest novel, *In Their Wisdom*. The darkness is still there, and illness and death, but they all are regarded now with a quiet, contemplative eye; the races have indeed been run and the prizes carried away; but things now take on a sober colouring from a mind made still by constant watch over man's mortality, though there is nothing of the Wordsworthian upsurge of feeling for the tenderness of the human heart.

Snow's personal gloom is expanded and elevated when set against the larger scientific and political movements in our century. I mentioned earlier that Rutherford's buoyancy epitomised the scientific spirit of the nineteen-thirties in Britain. But Rutherford and his school, borne on a tide of early success, themselves initiated a chain of discoveries which showed that the ultimate nature of matter was more complicated than they had at first suspected. At the fundamental level, nature revealed an element of chance and uncertainty which had to be incorporated into scientific philosophy and into the very fabric of scientific theory. While scientific discovery surged ahead more strongly than ever before, the newly gained philosophical perspectives inevitably coloured man's view of the universe and of life in it as entirely governable. Some of the early exuberance naturally diminished.

At the same time, science and technology were bringing about radical changes. The discoveries about the nature of the atom ultimately led to nuclear fission; and the bomb changed world politics profoundly and irreversibly. Science and government became interlinked. It was hoped, somewhat naïvely, that the rational methods of science could be applied to the art of government, but in spite of the increasing participation of scientists in government, that expectation has been largely unfulfilled. Snow's early recognition of this is manifest in *Corridors of Power,* where the paranoiac irrationality of the scientist Brodzinski helps to drown Roger Quaife's sane voice asking for disarmament. Outside their laboratories, scientists have shown themselves to be as subject to prejudice and irrationality as those who do not make a profession of reasoned argument and experiment. If so highly competent a scientist as Brodzinski can be so deaf to reason and, at the same time, so powerful that he cannot be left out of key decisions, there is little hope that the Quaife-Getliffe combination will be truly effective in the act of government.

While scientific and technological research went ahead rapidly, its consequences had raced beyond control. Adam Sedgwick, a character in the novel *In Their Wisdom,* seems to stand partly for the grotesque ineffectuality of the scientist in the world of the seventies. In the ensuing chapter on style, I do indeed state that Snow, for the most part, deliberately avoids symbolism. However, the point of view of *In Their Wisdom,* Olympian in its perspective, hovers over the people scattered below so detachedly and broodingly that the characters quietly take on wider connotations, link themselves to larger issues than they usually do in Snow's novels. Sedgwick, brilliant scientist and member of the House of Lords, has Parkinson's disease; he trembles with no control over his movements, his face convulsed by twitches, his hands quivering. And when he moves, his walk is distorted to the point of being ludicrous, 'a run-and-shuffle to the door, bent over at an angle of forty-five degrees, centre of gravity in advance of his feet, like an old style music hall comedian coming on to the stage.'[1] Only his mind remains as keen as ever, 'one of the most lucid minds extant'. Sedgwick quite effectively condenses in his person the grotesquerie reached by modern science. The uncontrollable shaking of Adam Sedgwick and his superbly active mind together hint at the state of science in the modern world – almost comically ineffectual at the same time that it is admirably impressive. We might reiterate that he is a member of the Upper House of Parliament. But the one speech we see him making there, however crisp its thought, embarrasses those listening to the 'fumbles of his tongue',[2] as this disabled man attempts vainly to convey his coherent and brisk argument. This is a fine symbol of the breakdown in communication between those who think and those who rule.

Science and government? For all that Snow demands, in his Godkin lectures of that name, that there should be more scientists in high places, he himself knows too much about government to be quite convinced that the Brodzinskis and Lindemanns can be shut out. Certainly he does not convince us. What he does succeed in doing is to create an ambivalent response in the reader, rising doubtless from an ambivalence in the writer himself – admire that it *may* be thus while bleakly realising that it is, in fact, otherwise.

Last Things also takes account of the horrifying consequences of the immense strides taken by biology and chemistry in the early fifties when the key to heredity seems to have been found. The discontent and disillusion of young people a decade later when they discover that such knowledge can be used to exterminate life is accurately recorded in the quixotic zeal of young Charles Eliot and his friends as they attack a university laboratory suspected of conducting research on biological warfare.

The subtle psychology of the Cold War brought its own morality of permissiveness and near-despair, when the young had to fight wars not of their own making, for causes they sympathised little with, using weapons directly evolved out of the scientific research of their parents' generation. To men like Snow, who lived through the buoyancy of the thirties in Cambridge, the fruits of their action must have indeed tasted bitter.

In addition to recognising the changing, less hopeful view of science, Snow confronts also the collapse of the liberal ideal. Unquestionably, in the period just before the Second World War, liberals, disillusioned by the growth of authority in Germany, turned increasingly towards communism, not fully realising the extremes to which authoritarianism could be carried by those who championed the workers. Their eventual oppressiveness struck a blow at the very roots of the freedom so dear to the liberal faith, a blow from which it has not yet recovered.

Another reason for its failure is that it drew into itself a motley crowd among whom the scientists and the lower-class poor are only two elements. As a result of its own inchoate and diverse nature, it could not make its utopia a practicable, realisable one. While admitting that Snow's symbols do not rise readily from his language, we might recognise, as in the case of Adam Sedgwick, that there is an overall symbolism in the failure of George Passant. He too is made up of far too many diverse elements – social rebelliousness, high idealism, sensual indulgence, self-delusion, charismatic touches – to emerge as a harmonious human being, let alone a social leader.

But liberalism, along with world events, left its mark on the old Conservative school of thought, which, willy-nilly, had to soften, open its windows and let the winds of change blow through its rooms. Sir Hector Rose's support of Roger Quaife in *Corridors of Power* and, more significantly, the fact that it is Quaife, a *Conservative* minister, who presses disarmament, are Snow's recognition of change. But despite this, the scales are depressed by the overall failure of Snow's political faith.

The partial breakdown of faith in science and liberalism is accompanied by a sad sense that unreason is stirring anew all over the Western world. The defeat of Roger Quaife's disarmament policy indicates the beginnings of a world in which reason does not dominate. It is obvious to all intelligent and humanitarian men that nuclear war is horrible, and yet they are not willing to take the path of right action. The minds of men cannot be manipulated even with the strongest will and the best intentions in the world. Snow adopts the Tolstoyan view of history here:

no matter who the individuals are, the course of events is not influenced by them. The tide in the affairs of men goes its own way. On the other hand, if one takes the tide at the flood, *personally* it may lead on to fortune. If Roger Quaife had waited another ten years, he may have become Prime Minister. But Quaife or no Quaife, historical events turn out as they will.

What disconcerts Lewis Eliot at this stage is the discovery of how little anyone can do for the social good. A supporter of Roger Quaife in the Ministry, he resigns after the policy is defeated. It is an open admission that he can do no more in the world of action. This is the last novel where Eliot appears in the thick of affairs. Henceforward, though he still has certain responsibilities, he is largely an observer, a looker-on.

What he sees gives little cause for reassurance. In the next novel, *The Sleep of Reason,* the gloom has gathered very considerably. Poverty has been banished, more or less, but the accompanying freedom, when taken to extremes, is appalling. Affluence and leisure for what ends? In a society where reason sleeps, these are dangerous and horrifying. Checks and limitations, restraints and the need to work, even a measure of want – these are surely preferable to a freedom that knows no limits and is accompanied by the means to do *whatever one likes.* Lewis Eliot in middle age comments sadly:

> Reason was very weak as compared with instinct. Instinct was closer to the aboriginal sea out of which we had all climbed. Reason was a precarious structure. But, if we didn't use reason to understand instinct, then there was no health in us at all.[3]

The last line falters with lack of conviction and the writer, like his character Eliot, is left standing on a desolate rock while the waves of unreason from 'the aboriginal sea' appear to sweep away his familiar landmarks.

The waning of Britain's political power is a very obvious background for a darkening perspective. *In Their Wisdom* presents the vote on the Common Market. Excitement runs high but Lord Ryle (who in some senses is a spokesman for the author), while clear that he must vote in favour of entering the European economic community, is emotionally not quite at one within himself on this matter:

> Was it his historian's training, was it temperament, was it, curiously enough, not being an aristocrat or an intellectual patrician that tied him to the past more than they were tied?[4]

Ryle and his friend Hillmorton escape the celebrations after the vote is taken, and the mood, for Ryle, is touched with nostalgia:

> Over the river was a temperate, misty, wistful autumn night and Ryle looked back to the celebrations.[5]

The night air itself and Ryle's backward-looking gesture prepare us for the overt homesickness of the close. As they walk slowly down Downing Street, 'thoughts drifting through their minds', the author tells us that Ryle did not recollect an acquaintance asking him, back in the thirties, whether he realised this was the most important street in the world. And he comments:

> That hadn't in cold fact been true then. At one time, at one privileged time, it might have been. It wouldn't be true again.
>
> All that, those two had accepted long ago. You came to terms. They had been coming to terms those last two days. You didn't overstay your welcome, or pretend for ever that you were stronger than you were. And yet, though Hillmorton hid it, there was regret somewhere in their mood.[6]

So much for the scientific and political shadows. What of the social scene? Snow may be no Hebrew prophet denouncing a mammon-worshipping age that has forgotten God, but he squarely confronts a materialistic society dazzled by money, and succeeds in disturbing our equanimity. He shows how there is not any more control over this than over science or politics. Fortunes are bequeathed to people with no real claim to them, passing over the true inheritors. Underwood's inheritance of £400,000 is a microcosmic version of the unpredictable shifts of money that have occurred all over the globe.

Snow comments that most people did not want to face how much they cared or worried about money; they would have liked loftier motives, but plainly it affects contemporary human life very profoundly:

> A visitor from another civilisation wouldn't have been illusioned or disillusioned, but he would have picked out one simple theme. Most men thought about money more than they admitted, and badly wanted it. The only thing they wanted more, perhaps, was that other men shouldn't have more money than themselves: or ideally should have less.[7]

Snow goes on to say that, in spite of this preoccupation with money, most men, especially the tender-minded, 'had hankerings after a different life'.[8] But there is little by way of choice. Religion is no longer a serious, credible alternative. 'Foraging among the money claims'[9] becomes, then, an all-absorbing pursuit.

True, in the earlier novels, he has portrayed struggles for power and success, also mammonistic goals, but idealism had not been quite ruled out. Time was when Roy Calvert would have shrugged indifferently over his chances of a sinecure, or Martin Eliot renounced the very position he had coveted and worked for. But now worldliness, unredeemed by any higher strain, stands drawn in the character of Julian Underwood, who assumes as his right what an earlier generation won with labour.

The characterisation of this man is the clearest indication of the extent to which Snow's vision (however calm his mind) has darkened. I can think of no other character in his novels from whom his sympathy has been so withdrawn. Till now, even the rogues were patiently explained and humanised. Jack Cotery, Charles Sheriff, for all their unscrupulousness, were likeable people. But Julian Underwood is not really of their company. He is horrifying because he is incapable of feeling, a type we have not encountered before in the world of Snow's novels. He is not shown as doing anything wicked or even wrong; he does not even openly show that he is avaricious. But he is in too perfect control of himself, cool and unaffected, while the contest over the will and huge fortune is coldly fought out. He has, rightly speaking, no claim whatsoever to the money, wangled for him out of a senile old man by his doting mother, by-passing a daughter's rights. The daughter, Jenny Rastall, and her inarticulate lover, Lorimer, are gentle, decent people, but how weak they are, how ineffectual in this world of money. One is reminded of the ineffectuality of Celia in *Volpone*.

When his lawyer presses him to accept the out-of-court settlement after the first judgement about the will has gone against him, Underwood makes his own cool calculations, decides to appeal, has his way though his lawyers think he is crazy, and *wins*. This is the crowning part and it leaves us unaccountably depressed. Lord Ryle concludes, after watching Underwood during the court hearings that he had not, in all his life, met a man 'so cool, so unifluenceable':

> This man was self-absorbed, not affected by others, but constantly aware of his effect on them and good at using it. He was solipsistic, if you like, no feeling except for himself, but nerves responding to the women round him, sensitive to sensations. That was a powerful combination. It was obvious enough that he basked cool and sultan-like, in domination.[10]

It is difficult to pinpoint any single reason why Julian Underwood shocks the reader; an impression of self-centredness builds itself up from his wide-eyed looks, his sudden bursts and hoots of hilarity, his finger to the side of his nose, his use of 'Mummy' to his mother (the man is in his early forties), his refusal to commit himself to his adoring mistress, Liz Hillmorton, his fretfulness about death-duties on an estate that, under usual and normal circumstances, should certainly never have come to him. He is so blandly courteous and charming, so supremely good-looking and poised, so completely unflappable; but behind it all one senses a corruption, hardness of heart and strength of will which, when combined, unnerve and repel. Here is Iago in modern dress, an Iago who does not even trouble to do evil but is simply there, corrupting the air around. We sense that his imperturbable surface hides a frightful emptiness which he neither knows nor cares about.

Snow remarks elsewhere in the novel in another context: 'There wasn't much stamina of the soul: there was almost infinite stamina of the ego',[11] an observation equally applicable to Underwood's self-centredness. For almost the first time in a Snow novel there is no humanisation of personality.

The coarse-grained, contemptuous doctor, Pemberton, is almost as shocking though the raw vulnerability beneath his rough and unpleasant surface softens him somewhat. Underwood, much more charming and light, is given no such saving grace. His mother and his mistress are shown pursuing heaven-knows-what shades of emotion as they fight over the affection he does not give.

On the sphere of personal relations also, then, the novel casts a desolating light. Lord Ryle, in his sixties, is given up to sensual and emotional reverie as he broods over the fact that 'sex didn't cut off clean, as the young liked to think. Maybe it didn't cut off at all'.[12] He falls in love with Liz Hillmorton who is eating her heart out for Julian Underwood. Jenny Rastall, a high-spirited, passionate woman, settles for the tongue-tied Lorimer, a good enough type, but hardly her match. The author comments on how well Jenny and Ryle would have suited each other if only they had met. On one occasion they are very near it, but Ryle is summoned by the division bell in the House of Lords and goes off to vote just before Jenny is introduced to him.[13] Random chance plays its part in determining human relationships. The author comments:

> The chances of possible partners whom one met produced a sense of fatality: so ought the chances of possible partners whom one didn't meet. The division bell had rung just as Ryle was about to be introduced to Jenny Rastall. As it happened, and it was pure chance, they didn't speak to each other that night, and were not to meet again until it was too late, though they would see each other across a room .... From their habits, affections, tastes and natures ... it seems more likely than not that they could have fitted one another: certainly more completely than with anyone they actually found.[14]

We have travelled a long way from the firm romantic faith of *Homecomings,* where Lewis Eliot and Margaret Davidson no sooner looked but they loved, and crossed over immense obstacles, including a marriage and child, to come to one another. The confidence that life can be thus manipulated has ebbed in the writer; increasingly he takes account of the imponderables.

There is no strong note of fulfilment in *In Their Wisdom*; most of the characters are prey to different anxieties, vainly pursuing chimeras. The pursuit of love has been a favourite Snow thesis, but here it is handled with a difference. Liz Hillmorton's hungering for Underwood strikes us as slightly demeaning, for we are told:

Underneath, in her longings, there was something not so much tender as abject.[15]

If such a 'nice' woman as this can lose her heart and head over such a man, what is the meaning at all of love? Equally, his mother's manoeuvring a huge fortune for him out of a sick old man, hoping to buy his affection therewithal, is slightly degraded.

The vanity of all human wishes is brought home through Lord Hillmorton's cancer and superbly underplayed death:

> Analgesics every four hours. Analgesics didn't give him much help, his nervous system appeared to have unusual resistance. Finally they used one which softened the pain but made him slobbery, merry and giggling like a fatuous cheery drunk.
>
> Presumably Hillmorton had once had some sort of dignity. This way of dying didn't leave one any dignity. Fancy giggling on the last stretch.[16]

What is the use of money, title, love, elegance, power, if all lessons must be reduced to this?

One is in danger of overstating one's case. There is a moment, a very real one, of fulfilment when Sedgwick, after brain surgery has been done on him, is able to move his hand and arm in a controlled way, an astonishing victory over Parkinson's disease:

> It was a moment of communion. You didn't need to take a lofty view of human beings, you could take one as contemptuous as Dr. Pemberton's, to recognise that it was a moment of selflessness. Their pleasure was unique and pure. Later on, maybe, Tompkin would be less pure, as he thought about his own credit: conversely, the other surgeon might reflect that he needed one of the star operations for himself. But not now. They were all united in a kind of species loyalty. Viscera, mind and spirit were at one. A sick man was better. Something had been done. Life was shining bright, and they were happy.[17]

The triumph of the operation on Sedgwick and the shared unselfish joy in the lines quoted take us back to two themes that have always loomed large in Snow's outlook: the hope for life held out by the reasoning methods of science, and brotherly love or a sense of shared humanity.

But the victory is an isolated one and it does not quite dispel the overall gloom. Swaffield is crass, Sedgwick, till almost the end, shakes like an aspen leaf, Hillmorton dies, Lord Lorimer looks foolish and keeps silent, the splendid Symingtons are struck by illness, Julian Underwood wins – all in all, we are made to feel the truth of the remark in the TLS review of the book that Snow's rational bridges are built over an abyss.

Patrick Swinden, in an excellent article in the *Critical Quarterly,* in discussing the 'indifferent dark' to which Snow is prey, declares that a tragic, absurd *and* human novel is a contradiction in terms. He feels that Snow has not adequately represented the inner life:

> The fact is that Snow does evince particular interest in this unsocial self, this mysterious repository of energy and suffering, of creative power and tragic depression. But it refuses to disclose itself in the plots he has discovered, the plots that suit the other social life so well.[18]

Swinden is one of the few critics who has given Snow credit for apprehending the 'essential loneliness of life, of its absurd precariousness and its inevitable end', even while he criticises Snow's lack of success in connecting outer and inner. Most criticism of Snow's fiction hitherto has addressed itself to the surface life he excels in evoking. One might reiterate strongly that below the surface there courses what one might call 'the buried life', after Matthew Arnold's poem of that name, in which, despite 'all the thousand nothings of the hour', melancholy echoes come as from an infinitely distant land, upborne from the soul's subterranean depth. The two streams, the stupefying demands of the hour, and the stresses of the hidden life, are finely illustrated in even as early a novel as *The Light and the Dark* (the least hopeful of all Snow's early work), where Roy Calvert, after considerable opposition from other Fellows and many ups and downs in the electoral process, is finally in the chapel taking his oath following his election as a Fellow:

> Roy knelt in the Master's stall, his palms together, the Master's hands pressing his. The clear light voice could be heard all over the chapel, as he took the oath. The Master said the final words, and began shaking Roy's hand. As we moved forward to congratulate him, Brown nudged me and whispered: 'Now I really do believe that fate can't touch us.'[19]

Brown is referring to the fact that, after a great deal of trouble, Roy has been securely elected. But the reader, who has by now understood Roy's spiritual affliction and the way fate has not just touched but caught, trapped him, cannot help applying the words ironically to Roy's inner life. Elsewhere in the novel Eliot refers to 'the essence of our nature' which lies within us, 'untouchable by our own hands or any others, by any chance of things or persons, from the cradle to the grave',[20] the hidden self, sealed off in a 'dimension of its own'. And of the ensuing isolation, he comments: '. . . for he was he, and I was I, as Montaigne said, and so we knew each other.'[21]

Snow appears to think freedom ultimately may only be an appearance, but it is an appearance we must take to be reality if a semblance of meaning is to emerge at all. Of Roy Calvert Eliot says:

He would be swept like this all through his life; at times, as now, he would be driven without will; he would not have *the appearance of will which gives life dignity, meaning and self-respect.*[22]

For most of his life Eliot holds fast to that 'appearance of will', but near-ly thirty years later he is still unconvinced that there is anything more than an illusion of freedom. As the lawyers argue back and forth about the two murderers of eight-year-old Eric Mawby, Eliot reflects:

Free choice, Who had a free choice? Did any of us? We felt certain that we did. We had to live as if we did. It was an experiential category of our psychic existence . . .. We had to believe that we could choose. Life was ridiculous unless we believed that. Otherwise there was no dignity left – or even no meaning. And yet – we felt certain we could choose, were we just throwing out our chests against the indifferent dark? We had to act as if it were true. As if. *Als/ob.* That was an old answer. Perhaps it was the best we could find.[23]

In the earlier novel Eliot had suspected that such might be the nature of truth, but he had half believed that Roy's doom could possibly have been brought on by his own nature, that the actual events of our lives, despite the unalterable natural endowment within, could be affected by the choice of our will. By the time of *The Sleep of Reason,* from which the last lines are taken, he is quite convinced that life is absurd and freedom and will but words.

None of this cancels out what was said in Chapter 1 about Snow belonging with the contemporaries rather than the moderns, for nowhere does he give in to despair or feel himself cut off completely from tradition and the past. He is not shaken to the very marrow as the modern is, but pessimism and darkness seep in slowly over the years making for an increasingly stoical attitude on his part.

We see that the humanistic faith of the intervening novels has been tried in the balance and found wanting; yet Snow cannot give it up altogether for there is no other prop to hold on to; the bridge of his faith sways perilously over the 'aboriginal' swirl below but at least it keeps him from plunging into the waters of despair, from quite going over to the modernist position.

From beneath all the busy action of self-important men: dons, lawyers, treasury officials – the whole crowd, echoes float upward from the 'indifferent dark', questioning, doubting; shadowy clouds streaming into the day of Snow's carefully built palace of reason. He almost seems to hold his hands to his ears to keep himself from hearing the question: 'what then?', but apparently he does not quite succeed. We can only ad-mire his honesty in acknowledging forces which make nonsense of his beliefs, and the stoic acceptance with which, in true English fashion, he *carries on.* Not only that, we have to admit that the growing pessimism adds an aesthetic dimension to the world of his fiction. The reader's need for an evocation of whatever goes beyond the surface reckoning is partially satisfied by this sadness. Hope, after all, flaps a tinsel wing. The fitful melancholy strains sound not simply touching but inevitable as his novels sweep to a darkening close.

6 Characterisation and style

Edmund Fuller in an article on Snow comments pertinently on an important aspect of his method of characterisation:

> Snow as novelist can see all around a man, as one might walk around a Henry Moore sculpture, noting its holes and distortions, but also its proportions and solidities.[1]

This habit springs from his deeply-felt need to understand human nature as fully as possible. The overall title given to his long sequence, *Strangers and Brothers,* sums up perfectly his attitude: to know all *is* to understand all. Such receptivity has an inevitable influence on his craft of characterisation, especially on the drawing of his major characters, for it leads him to discard the traditional devices of heightening and exaggeration. Selection of detail, essential for aesthetic impact, becomes in consequence a tricky and difficult affair. We must know a great deal about everybody if we are to love and forgive them all. I believe that, in the case of the dominating central characters, Snow pays the aesthetic price for not being able to make that selection; the impact gets muffled; we are nowhere stabbed broad awake. On the other hand, the deliberate inclusiveness, though it takes away sharpness of outline; sinks into the reader's mind and changes his mode of perceiving people, making him gradually less fanatical, less willing to judge and condemn. With the minor characters, the effect is quite different, for Snow here wants to leave a vivid mark, and he manages to do so quite successfully by resorting to the conventional method of heightened and slightly exaggerated detail.

The fourteen serious novels that Snow has written may be divided into three groups. First, there are the novels in which a single character dominates the action and is explored in great detail by the writer. Such heroes are Arthur Miles in *The Search,* George Passant in *Strangers and Brothers* (now re-titled *George Passant*), Roy Calvert in *The Light and the Dark,* Charles March in *The Conscience of the Rich,* and Lewis Eliot in *Time of Hope* and *Homecomings.* Second, there are the novels in which there is indeed a central major character, but he is not developed with quite the same passionate scrutiny as the heroes of the first group. In these novels issues and events share as much of the novelist's interest as the protagonists themselves. Such heroes are Martin Eliot in *The New Men,* Roger Quaife in *Corridors of Power* and Lewis Eliot in *Last Things.* Third, there are the novels which have no readily identifiable major characters, but are instead peopled by a large number of men and women surveyed by the author with a detached eye. Such novels are *The Masters, The Affair, The Sleep of Reason, The Malcontents* and *In Their Wisdom.*

It is worth remarking that the novels without all-important central figures were all (with the exception of *The Masters*) written in Snow's later period, dating from the fifties. One might surmise from this that, by that time, Snow's passion for in-depth exploration of the inner drama of personalities had spent itself. He seems in recent years to work on a larger canvas with larger numbers of people. *Last Things* is indeed a book of Lewis Eliot's direct experience, but he is not the central pivotal figure in it to the extent that he is in the two earlier books about himself, *Time of Hope* and *Homecomings.* Snow is now content to survey the scene and speculate about the figures dotted on it rather than get deeply involved with any of them. In the period from *The Sleep of Reason* to *The Malcontents* one can almost sense an onset of emotional exhaustion, as it were, on the part of the writer. In *Last Things* it expresses itself as a growing gloom in which the goings-on of the young, however sym- pathetically viewed, do not really touch the centre of the narrator's con- sciousness or affect his imagination as groups of people had in his earlier books. In *The Malcontents* Snow's interest in characters seems to have dropped away altogether. One reads it with some astonishment. Can these wooden people really be Snow's? It would appear that the author's interest in people had dried up for a while; instead, he seems to have been preoccupied with an abstraction of the zealous, idealistic young to the point where feeling, characterisation, even the reflective in- telligence, have all been thrown overboard.

But with the publication of *In Their Wisdom* the novelist seems to have regained his zest for people. A fine balance has been struck in this novel: the earlier detailed explorations have gone but the large number of characters who are introduced are handled with expertness and con- fidence. They come to life with surprising clarity though they are not much dwelt upon individually. The reflective analysis is back but it is used less for character development than for describing the process of life in general, the meaning of action and the quality of the historical moment. There is not any more hopefulness in this book than in *Last*

Things but the characterisation here shows a renewed self-assurance and vitality.

As remarked earlier, Snow is not wholly successful with his central, dominating characters. Some of them, notably Roy Calvert and, to a lesser extent, Martin Eliot, appear static; they grow and develop very little. George Passant comes off best, perhaps because his disintegration is traced through a number of books and, in the process, the gradual shifts and changes in his character can be observed.

With Roy Calvert, fascinated as Eliot seems to be by his problem, the static impression is dominant. Roy's manic-depressive state is described with loving care but we are not made to sense any growth within Roy himself. The premonition of his death dominates all his other activities right from the start. His hopelessness is too relentlessly borne in upon us by Eliot; hence the fixed, rigid nature of the characterisation. The Jonsonian humoural treatment of a character pinned by a typical trait, used by Snow with eminent success in his minor figures, seems not enough to underline the complexities of a central, leading character like Roy.

The partial failure in the characterisation of Martin Eliot in *The New Men* may be attributed to two possible reasons. First, he appears in a novel which is essentially without a hero. Too much is going on in the book for the novelist to expend much energy on Martin. The second reason is Martin's own inarticulateness. To cast him as such a character is valid enough but there is no full exploration of the fears and anxieties that undoubtedly underlie this man's taciturn personality. If there was too much introspection in *The Light and the Dark,* there is too little of it here. Or rather, the novel seems undecided about its main preoccupation – the busy business concerning the bomb, or the inner problems of the men who are making it. This is also the case in the political novel *Corridors of Power.* There are so many issues to be considered that the inner life of Roger Quaife is only very perfunctorily touched. Why, when he seems to be so happily married to a beautiful, aristocratic and devoted wife, is he having an affair with Ellen Smith? There has been no hint that the marriage is not what it seems on the surface – brilliant and satisfying; nor are there any suggestions that Quaife is an unusually susceptible man.

Charles March, the hero of *The Conscience of the Rich,* is better conceived and presented but even here a secondary character, his father, tends to overshadow him.

The most important of Snow's central characters is, of course, Lewis Eliot, narrator of the eleven novels within the sequence and the focus of experience in three of them. As a young man, he is shown as clever and gifted, especially in an academic sense. There is a ruthless streak in him that impels him to reject his mother's possessiveness and waste his best years pursuing a shadow, a relationship in which he alone can be the giver. He seems to be a person much loved by his friends but not very likeable at the core. There is a selfish hardness within about the things that are really important to him. In love with Sheila, he possibly wrecks her only chance of finding happiness and stability by sending away her lover. Infuriated by a junior's gossiping tongue, he promptly gets him transferred. Once he has realised the defects of his emotional nature, he is able to fight his egotism and possessiveness and draw his second wife into a circle of shared feeling. From now on, he has a centre of tranquillity and joy. Thus far he has emerged as a somewhat selfish and ambitious young man capable of strong feeling, still friendly and sensitive to other people, and pleasant in the outer layers of his personality. He has a good share of native impulsiveness and a great deal of acquired discretion. Politically, he is a liberal of leftist leanings, and he is aware of the danger that, as he becomes more comfortably ensconced in the Establishment, he may give up rebellion altogether. There was some danger after his new-found happiness in marriage that Eliot, having finally 'arrived' in all senses, would cease to grow and change. There were hints of such a standstill in the novels after *Homecomings* (such as *The Affair* and *Corridors of Power*) where contentment within the family seemed to have made him too serene within himself. But in the last novel of the sequence, *Last Things,* there is significant change, what Malcolm Bradbury in his brilliant essay calls 'a striking change of direction'.[2] With the onset of old age and illness his props falter: Margaret's voice after the operation seems very far away and not very relevant to Eliot's terror and loneliness when he hears about his cardiac arrest and near-brush with death. After surviving the ordeal he gives out the sense of a man exhausted by the struggle, puzzled by a world slipping from his grasp, puzzled by the younger generation, yet striving through his son to strike a balance and achieve a sense of continuity. It is a convincing end to Eliot's cycle from the high hope of youth to the bleak stoicism of old age.

The intention of the novelist in his creation of Lewis Eliot is clear enough but the success of the characterisation itself is another question. There is a thinness, a bloodlessness, a lack of immediacy about Lewis Eliot that make it impossible for us to know him in the way we know the secondary and minor characters in the novel. The fact is, though we know all *about* Lewis Eliot, we do not know the man himself. This may be because it is impossible for him, telling his own story, to convey distinguishing tricks of speech and gesture. His dialogue is never long; after a line or two, Snow will go back to reported speech in his case. As a result we seldom hear him and we never can visualise him, for, of course, he rightly cannot describe himself. Some dimension seems to be lacking. Bergonzi attributes this largely to the first-person narrative technique of the whole series. The difficulty, he says, with a first-person narrator is that 'he will be unable to describe naturally and convincingly

his own deepest emotional experiences: in such cases, a note of em-
barrassment nearly always intrudes.'[3] However, other first-person
narrators in fiction have not all been so curiously impersonal as Lewis
Eliot. One thinks of David Copperfield, Jane Eyre, even the unnamed
narrator in Daphne du Maurier's novel *Rebecca*. The reason, I believe,
for the partial failure of Lewis Eliot in making full emotional impact on
the reader is that the author gives too much analysis of his character and
too little of physical concrete description to fill him out, We get a clearer
impression of Jane Eyre, on the other hand, because we can hear her
talk. Her own conversation in direct speech and her fervent appeals to
the reader illuminate the passionate nature underlying her small, in-
significant person. In the case of David Copperfield there is no emptiness because there is more projection of himself by the narrator and
less analysis. Pamela Hansford Johnson notes that partly Lewis Eliot
does not come to life because the serious aspect alone predominates.
She says:

> We have seen George wholly and Sheila wholly, but Lewis only in
> part. The reticence so ingrained in his character has . . . operated only
> in one direction, to minimise the lighter side, the aspect of the per-
> sonality displayed in the lighter intimacies, which is an aspect not to
> be dismissed as negligible because it is the aspect from which the
> world judges in the long run, makes its casual and enduring
> judgements.[4]

While as a character in the conventional sense Lewis Eliot seems to have a
side missing, as an ever-present disembodied voice and a filtering sensibility he becomes slowly a very real presence to the reader. This is not
only because he has been with us so long, but because we see that sensibility taking certain steadfast attitudes of liberal decency and holding
on to them through a rapidly changing world. That hold towards the
end is admittedly somewhat precarious but this only makes the
characterisation in this special sense more real and touching. What we
see in the life of Lewis Eliot is a recapitulation of how the pressures of
our age fashioned and bent one particular mind holding a particular set
of beliefs. In a less obvious sense, therefore, the characterisation of
Lewis Eliot has not failed altogether. The relationship of Lewis Eliot to
the world around him has been successfully drawn.

The characterisation of young Charles Eliot, Lewis Eliot's son, stands
apart. He is not a major character in his own right nor can he be treated
as a minor character, but in his portraiture, it seems to me, Snow has
been eminently successful. His conversation is beautifully handled, its
tone and content entirely in keeping with his period – the cool, well-
informed idealism of the students of the late sixties. A comparison of the
sketch of this bright young man with the much earlier Roy Calvert is il-

luminating. In both cases the characters are obviously creations for whom the writer has great affection. But Snow is content to let young Charles speak for himself, briefly and casually, without the excessive overt analysis which almost overwhelmed the delineation of Roy Calvert. The emotion, very deeply felt in both cases, is here held firmly reined.

Snow's minor characters seem to me to be much his best. Through them he manages to communicate an impression of the variegatedness of modern life. Around the bleak and sober central characters we see crowds of people pursuing various professions: scientists, industrialists, dons, lawyers, civil servants, doctors and clergymen. All of them contribute to the 'hum and buzz of life' through which the major figures move. They come alive for us partly because they are sketched with a lighter touch. Their tricks of speech and mannerisms throw them into relief and Snow's speculations about their inner nature are sharp and brief, and surprisingly illuminating. They are largely types, fixed by a habit.

These minor characters may be grouped into several broad classes or types: the bureaucratic; the politically idealistic; the scientifically high-minded; the failed and embittered, the confident and complacent; women who are simple and single-minded or fine-grained and imaginative; the tricky and elusive; the hypersensitive; the raw-edged and raw-nerved.

Of the bureaucratic men who are chained to their desks the very early sketch of Mr Vesey in *Time of Hope* stands out for its Dickensian vividness. He disappears for ever after a page or two, but enough has been said for us to understand the pressures felt by this tormented clerk whose life is governed by the prospect of promotion and who sees any fresh talent as a threat to his own advancement. His neurotic anxiety to please his superiors reappears many years later in a civil servant called John Jones in *Homecomings* but now under a more decorous and polished veneer.

In the upper rungs of the bureaucratic hierarchy Snow gives us the civil servants, Hector Rose and Douglas Osbaldistone, the cool, fair and highly competent types with machine-like minds, trained and sharpened by a rigorous education. Part of Snow's originality lies in the authenticity of creations such as these, who do not in life leave the vivid air signed with their honour, who do not even linger in our memory through grotesque or eccentric habits, but who come home to our imagination as people we have certainly known but not heretofore thought very much about. When we hear in *Last Things* that solid, middle-aged Sir Hector Rose has married an alluring young creature, we are happy, and we realise, somewhat to our surprise, that affection for this sound, sensible though not highly imaginative man has been subtly inspired in us by the writer.

Of the scientific, high-minded types, Francis Getliffe, Mounteney and Constantine are examples. About all of them there is a certain impatience with the ordinary conduct of affairs, a touch of being above it all, and a thin-skinned irritability with more 'broad-bottomed' men. Francis Getliffe is an important marginal figure through most of the novels and his death in *Last Things* sounds a distinct farewell note to the progressive, scientific attitude he stood for, an attitude Snow regretfully sees as disappearing from the scene in the seventies. He undoubtedly represents the buoyant and exciting mood of English science in the thirties and forties, and his confidence in his rightness is an indication of the tremendous faith of British science in itself during that period. For this reason he is not explored much as a person; his fears and uncertainties are never revealed.

Despard-Smith, Fane and Winslow are examples of the failed, embittered types, each with a different degree of rancour. Of the simple single-minded women Lady Muriel is an epitome of the unmitigated snob, Mrs Knight of the devoted wife, and Rosalind of the alluring adventuress who really wants marriage. Margaret Davidson and Joan Royce are more sensitive and refined. Mr Knight, with his languid air and his superb voice and diction, is the hypersensitive man too proud to compete in the world, yet acutely interested in it.

Of the tricky, elusive type Herbert Getliffe, the lawyer, is one of the best of all Snow's minor characters. Herbert Getliffe is a successful barrister, slightly unscrupulous and always slightly muddled, but with an unfailing sense for the main line of the argument and with considerable presence in court. The subtleness with which Snow defines this kind of impact, very unlike that of the formidable and stately personality, is impressive indeed. He suggests that muddiness of mind can coexist with acumen, and that Herbert Getliffe's fluidity of personality and his own brand of articulateness, neither flamboyantly rhetorical nor studiously understated, can affect a jury quite successfully. When Getliffe defends Eliot's friend George Passant, Eliot remarks of his final speech in court:

> It was in his usual style, spasmodic, still bearing the appearance of nervousness, interjected with jerky asides, ill-at-ease and yet familiar; he was showing all the touch which made men comfortable with him. He was showing also the fresh enjoyment which seldom left him when he was on his feet in court.[5]

Lewis Eliot and Charles March, both eager and bright young pupils, do not recognise this at once for they overvalue intelligence and clarity which they find missing in Getliffe. Eliot later realises that

> Getliffe's mind was muddy, but he was a more effective lawyer than men far cleverer because he was tricky and resilient, because he was

expansive with all men, because nothing restrained his emotions, and because he had a simple, humble, tenacious love for his job.[6]

Besides analysing Getliffe's untidy, magpie-like mind, Snow fills out the characterisation with convincing and authentic physical touches. When we see him for the first time he appears slightly flustered, and bustles in dragging his feet, his underlip thrust out in an affable grin. He is extravagant with his words, slides readily out of promises and is without much conscience. He sends his pupil Eliot no case to handle on his own while always declaring his intention of so doing. He uses Eliot's notes verbatim in his own arguments and makes his acknowledgements in a very obtuse and indirect way:

> Perhaps one ought to mention the help one sometimes gets from one's pupils. Of course one suggests a line of investigation, one reads their *billet-doux,* one advises them how to express themselves. But you know as well as I do, gentlemen, that sometimes these young men do some of the digging for us. Why, there's one minor line of argument in this opinion – it's going too far to say that I shouldn't have discovered it, in fact I had already got my observations in black and white, but I was very glad indeed, I don't mind telling you, when my Mr. Ellis hit upon it for himself.[7]

Later on, in *The Conscience of the Rich* we are not surprised to hear that Herbert Getliffe has dabbled somewhat improperly in financial speculations and that the shadows of scandal are gathering about him. There is a vivid glimpse of him in the midst of his troubles. Yet he remains an oddly engaging character – mercurial, gay and alive. Snow has drawn two other such practised, roguish figures: Charles Sheriff in *The Search* and Jack Cotery in the *Strangers and Brothers* sequence. Julian Underwood, of Snow's latest novel, *In Their Wisdom,* is far more sophisticated and hard-hearted while still retaining the unscrupulous qualities of the earlier roguish types.

We can see a growth in Snow's art of characterisation inasmuch as his people are less typical and more complicated in the later novels. He remarked in the *REL* interview that he was interested not only in the typical essence but also in the surprises of character, the unpredictable streaks.[8] He demonstrates his ability to re-create the surprises of character especially in the figure of Thomas Pemberton in *In Their Wisdom.* Pemberton is a doctor, the heir to Lord Hillmorton's title. A scornful, inflexible and uncultivated man, he typifies both the efficiency of scientific training and the lack of subtlety that may accompany it. Pemberton displays an emotional poverty, a lack of gentleness, somehow linked with his busy medical rounds. He rushes from clinic to surgery to home without pausing to care about the feelings of other people though he attends to their illnesses with irreproachable efficiency. He regards emotions as luxuries and doubts their validity. At the same time, he is himself a seething mass of feelings which he has not ever recognised. Because he has nothing of the introspective habit, he does not see his reaction to Lord Hillmorton for the angry resentment that it is. When he had needed money as a young man, he had approached Hillmorton only to be snubbed and made aware of his low background. So he waits and watches without pity as his distant and despised but aristocratic kinsman dies of cancer. His contact at the hospital keeps him secretly informed of the last stages of the illness, and Pemberton has his letter claiming his title ready to mail even before Hillmorton is dead.

This is not so much a picture of the practical man of action as it is a portrait of a man who has no gentleness and no cultivation. The effect is raw and repelling. And yet, it is not as simple as that either. Within himself, Pemberton, however he might pooh-pooh the ceremonious and beautiful, is insecure in the House of Lords. He does not like feeling outclassed. And when Elizabeth Hillmorton snubs him even as her father did, he feels hot hate starting up:

> Pemberton, enraged, felt as violent as when young, and could have smashed her teeth in. He felt he was being snubbed, which was true, and snubbed on social grounds, which wasn't.[9]

So much ego and so little awareness of it; so much assertiveness and so little confidence! But even in this brutal simple man we discover an unsuspected streak. He hears about Sedgwick; feels an unfamiliar emotion – respect – stirring; takes the trouble of introducing himself and visiting him in the hospital before his operation, and strikes up a curiously sympathetic, if rough-edged, relationship with him. Though Sedgwick makes it plain to Pemberton's questions about a possible career in medical research for himself that he is too old to do anything even decently second-rate, Pemberton finds, to his surprise, that he still cares about Sedgwick:

> To his own puzzlement, he was not objective about this piece of surgery. Not that he preserved any hope, or really had ever had any, that Sedgwick would help his old, slightly pathetic, scientific ambitions . . .. If that had been true, it would have been a good, sound, selfish, egotistic, realistic reason for being concerned about Sedgwick's condition. Pemberton would have understood himself for that, and have approved. But he had no such reason, and was still concerned. He respected Sedgwick. Surely that wasn't enough? After all, he was an old man, all he had done in science was already done. His effective life was over. In the nature of things, his physical life couldn't last very long. Pemberton had no use for people who got maudlin about mortality. Pemberton didn't like symptoms of maudlin sentiment in himself. Yet he was still concerned.[10]

In drawing Pemberton, Snow has been eminently successful in creating a cogent, complex whole: physical details ('built like a heavy-weight boxer'), capacity for rancour, overall impatience, brute confidence, rankling inner sense of inferiority, the odd and sudden sympathy for Sedgwick – all coalesce into a credible, living human being.

Reginald Swaffield, the immensely rich property developer, who heads a business empire is another character from *In Their Wisdom* who illustrates the development of Snow's characterisation. Though he is as vividly realised as the minor figures in the earlier novels, he is, like Pemberton, more than a type; yet, unlike the early central figures, he does not project a blurred image. And Snow hints at certain aspects of his personality which arouse our curiosity but which are not over-elaborated. His typical nature comes out in his love of power, evoked by his opulent home, his blustering manner, his fabulous parties and his employment of peers like Lord Clare whom he can fire at will. Paul Lufkin, of the *Strangers and Brothers* sequence, was not unlike this, though his surface appearance was different. In their love of the feel of power, both rich men are typical, influence-wielding millionaires. But Swaffield is developed further. Having acquired power and money, he now needs to manipulate people, arrange their fates, make them buckle under to the plans he has for them. This is why he takes up the case of Jenny Rastall whom he does not initially know personally. He spends thousands of pounds on lawyers' fees fighting Jenny Rastall's case against Julian Underwood. We are told that once, years ago, Mrs Underwood had slighted Swaffield; he was 'becoming an eminent as a tycoon – and she asked him what he did'. But this is only an acknowledged motive for a feeling that runs deeper:

> Swaffield did not forget snubs even when, perhaps particularly when, he had invented them. He let them breed, and gained much pleasure from paying them out, the longer afterwards, the more triumphant. Jenny didn't need to have any precise intimation of all that. The nerve showed through. But it was so sharp, it disguised from her a more in-teresting surgency beneath. She still had no conception what his kind of personal imperialism was like – nor how, if he had had no relation with Mrs. Underwood at all, he would nevertheless have been sitting with Jenny on his sofa that night, bullying her and taking charge of her affairs.[11]

Here is love of power taking a subtler form under the hectoring, restless crude surface of Swaffield's personality. When he goes on holiday he needs to take 'his court' with him; he is ready to pay for his whole company of guests.

> For Swaffield not only needed people around him, he needed people for – what? applause? recognition of debt? reminders of his power?[12]

That he certainly does not patronise Jenny because of any sexual tinge in their relationship is made abundantly clear. His love life is kept a close secret. At the end of a dinner party his foot taps with impatience, his eyes grow hot, because his guests have not departed:

> Those who had most to do with him suspected that he was expecting another visitor that night, or maybe there was another visitor already in the house. That aspect of Swaffield none of them knew. He enjoyed living everyone's ,lives in public, but there was one exception, his own.[13]

Snow leaves it at that. One of the striking features about characterisation in the later novels is that he does not explain too much. He hints at obliquites and is content to let gestures and physical details speak for themselves.

Snow's method of characterisation with most of his minor characters is old-fashioned. Mainly he relies on descriptions of external appearances, characteristic mannerisms of speech, the incidental comments of other characters and chiefly, for the novels within the sequence *Strangers and Brothers,* the comments of the narrator Lewis Eliot. People are firmly placed in their town and class and are given readily recognisable local habitations and names.

Snow's most effective way of making his characters memorable is through their speech. He has a finely tuned ear for the peculiarities of spoken style and tricks of speech. Both Roy Calvert and Charles March have favourite phrases of their own which they use again and again in their dialogue – a mannerism which serves to indicate a streak of anxiety that they have in common. For instance, Charles March has a habit of ending his observations with a question tag:

> . . . you did lose sight of the point for five minutes, didn't you? it was a classical example of using two arguments where one would do, don't you agree?[14]

or

> You haven't many ties, have you?[15]

or

> You're rather hoping he does know, aren't you?[16]

or

> It's that kind of discomfort he's frightened of, don't you admit it?[17]

or

> It means making a private plea, doesn't it?[18]

and so on. Roy Calvert has a similar anxiety tic of his own: the phrase 'just so'. Even more indicative of the relentless unrest within him is his 'I need' phrase. For example:

Just so. I need you to come.[19]

Again:

I need to give you some fresh air. I need to take you for a walk in the park.[20]

or

You look pretty worn. I need to order you some strawberries for tea.[21]

or

I need to say something to you. It's not easy.[22]

or

I don't know how I'm going to say it. I've needed to say it all night.[23]

or

There may come a time when I need to keep things from you.[24]

or, inviting Lady Muriel to play cards:

We need you to.[25]

Such conversational devices of characterisation are somewhat commonplace, but Snow uses them with a sure touch in building an ineradicable impression. Just as we come to recognise our friends by their tone of voice or the way they say a particular word, so too these characters come to live in our minds through their pet phrases and peculiar mannerisms. Arthur Brown, a cautious tutor at Cambridge, has a favourite expression in which the essence of discreet, mediocre but reliable fairness is pinned down: 'Put it another way.' Old Professor Gay, greedy with an old man's greed and heartiness, is likewise marked down by idiosyncratic words like 'spendid' 'absolutely' and 'congratulate the Steward for me'. We see these men age over a period of thirty years and hear their familiar phrases reverberate at each meeting. Snow, in doing this, is following the example of many novelists before him, especially Dickens, who excelled in the art of immortalising his characters by making them utter the unforgettable phrase: one remembers Uriah Heep, Barkis, Sam Weller. However, this technique has usually been used when the writer's intention is to satirise or ridicule or caricature. Even Galsworthy's James Forsyte (Soames's father) with his plaintive cry, 'Nobody ever tells me anything', is a slightly absurd figure. Snow, on the other hand, is using this method to reveal serious characters as well as ridiculous ones – Roy Calvert as well as Professor Gay.

Snow says significantly in his biography of Trollope that perhaps the most useful piece of technical resource a novelist can possess is a good ear or the ability to suggest in the dialogue the tone of spoken speech, and of each different person's spoken speech.[26] It seems to me that it is chiefly through his rendering of speech that Snow cuts close, to use the phrase of a *TLS* review, 'to the nerve-ends of his characters'. The words reveal whether those nerves are made of steel, as with Lady Boscastle, or frayed and agitated, as with Roy Calvert. I quote below a little vignette of Lady Boscastle from an early novel *The Light and the Dark*:

> 'If he's only a first secretary at forty I should not think he was going so terribly far.' Lady Boscastle directed her lorgnette at her husband. 'I remember one years younger. We were at Warsaw. Yes, he was clever.' A faint, sarcastic, charming smile crossed her face. Lord Boscastle smiled back – was I imagining it, or was there something humble, unconfident about that smile?[27]

The use of 'so terribly' and 'Yes, he was clever' catch unerringly her supreme confidence in herself, her tremendous style and sophistication. Lady Muriel, more a born aristocrat than Lady Boscastle but more of a bumbler, is not made to talk with anywhere near the same amount of self-assurance.

Julian Underwood's speech in the novel *In Their Wisdom* is another fine example of Snow's fine ear. Even though we have no detailed description of Julian Underwood, we seem to know astonishingly well both his excessively attractive physical appearance and his horrifying unfeelingness through his cool and deliberately casual words. The man who says:

> Do you know, Mummy, I've noticed before, that when anyone gets in my way they tend to come to a bad end?[28]

is the same one who frets about death duties to the mother who has secured him a fortune of £400,000:

> Couldn't you have done something about it? There must be ways of shedding the stuff. This is pretty fair incompetence, it must have been.[29]

Snow also makes use of the repeated detail in creating his character. Every time we meet Sir Hector Rose, Eliot will refer to his courteous bow and blinding politeness; every time we meet Helen Davidson we are made to notice her smart dress; old Mr March obsessively locks up the house for the night on a number of occasions; Julian Underwood has a wide-eyed look of openness at the very times he is being his shrewdest. These techniques of the repeated habit and the typical speech mannerisms fix the dominant impression in a way that reminds us of Jonson, though, as said earlier, his later characters like Pemberton and Swaffield go beyond such effects.

In the matter of attitude to people, and therefore in his attitude to his own characters, Snow is very unlike Jonson. Snow's deep-seated humanism and concern for men and women lead him to look at his fellow-beings primarily with a desire to understand them. This approach to people is an important factor in discussing Snow's characterisation for it determines partially its vividness or lack of it. Snow's dominant attitude is one of kindliness. If we recall Jane Austen for a moment and the remorseless light of her irony and wit, we can see in contrast that very few of Snow's characters are presented in such a manner. There is in Snow too much reluctance to judge and too strong an urge to probe, explain, and tentatively account for human behaviour. Nothing human is alien or shocking to him; he accepts the variety of human nature with gratitude and seldom sits in judgment. I believe that the compassionate desire to understand and explain human behaviour is carried by Snow further than many other novelists, and it impresses me as proceeding from a temperament as far removed from the fanatical as it is possible to be. Frederick Karl sharply observes that Lewis Eliot is capable of putting up with every kind of nonsense and seeing some value in every kind of fool.[30] On might perhaps retort that it is precisely this habit that is morally educative about Snow's fiction.

There is no spark of malice anywhere in his characterisation. That could, of course, lead to a dismal state of humourlessness but Snow does create some effective comic figures. Old Professor Gay, wonderfully vital octogenarian, and Mrs Henneker, writing the biography of her dead husband, provide a welcome hilarity in the midst of the serious reflectiveness. But the laughter is of a genial kindly sort, never really sharp. The scene in Anthony Powell's *Music of Time* of Widmerpool with a sugar-bowl inverted on his head would not be possible in Snow, for he explains too much to allow or even want such an effect.

While Snow's fairness and receptivity are marvellously impressive, they make for an evenness of tone which has led some critics to believe he is coldly analytic and detached. J. B. Priestley remarks of the people in *The New Men* that they are 'chilly and spectral, as if . . . we . . . were all flitting from one committee of ghosts to another'.[31] In a similar vein Brady speaks of the aridity and desiccation that accompany Snow's curiosity about characters.[32] The aridity, it appears to me, arises not from the writer's coldness towards people but from his deliberately cultivated reluctance to appeal to the senses.

But, as mentioned earlier, the evenness of tone has meant the sacrifice of heightening and distorting effects which usually sharpen characterisation. It is for this reason, I believe, that Snow resorts to Jonsonian techniques though he is himself so far from the Jonsonian view of life and men. If it were not for their external details and peculiarities of speech, his men and women would disappear behind a blur of explanations.

On the whole, it seems to me that Snow strikes a fair balance between external characterisation and cerebral speculations and explanations. As an example of the latter we might take an instance from *The Affair,* a novel in which Howard, a Cambridge scientist, has been possibly wrongly dismissed from his Fellowship on charges of scientific fraud. The college is split about whether or not the case should be reopened for investigation, and there are pro-Howard and powerful anti-Howard factions. Tom Orbell, a youngish history don who is not over-fond of the Howards decides, after considerable wavering, to join the party agitating for a reopening of the case. Lewis Eliot wonders why he changes his mind and joins them after all.

> We had known for minutes past, almost from his first question, that he was changing sides. But his tone was not what one might have expected. He kept some of his desire to please; he was trying to sound warm, to feel what most of us feel when we are giving our support. He did not manage it. He had thrown away his prudence, his addiction to keeping in with the top; but he had not done it out of affection for us. Nor out of devotion to Hanna. Nor out of the honour he was protesting about. Instead he seemed to be acting partly from direct feeling for a victim, partly from frustrated anger. One felt, under the good-living, self-indulgent, amiable surface, how violent he was to himself.[33]

Here, entirely through cool, flat analysis, Eliot attempts to penetrate to the core of Orbell's decision. A little of this, a little of that, wondering about the sharp edge in the tone and guessing at its springs – this is typical of Lewis Eliot's attempts at understanding the psychological sources of character throughout the whole *Strangers and Brothers* sequence.

While Snow is evidently interested in exploring the psychological 'within' of his characters, he does not re-create through evocation the psychological consciousness itself; nor does he make use of the uncontrolled subconscious beyond perhaps recognising that it may determine action and behaviour. Mrs Underwood's affection for her son Julian, for instance, in the novel *In Their Wisdom,* seems to me to have a streak of the yearning and passionate about it, though this is never openly acknowledged.[34] Quite inevitably she loathes her son's mistress, Elizabeth Hillmorton. But Snow neither uses any Freudian terms nor even suggests strongly the impulses of the subconscious in the way Angus Wilson does in *No Laughing Matter,* where the relationships between Mr Matthews and his daughter Gladys, and Mrs Matthews and her sons Rupert and Marcus are broadly and unmistakably drawn in Freudian terms.

Finally, we must take note of Snow's consistent refusal to see people in simplistic terms. He seems to see the different selves of a person as all equally part of him. In fact, he takes the attitude a step further and suggests that his characters become, in some cases, what they are perceived to be. George Passant with Jack Cotery (who is softly insinuating and unscrupulous) is different from the George Passant seen by Lewis Eliot, and different again from the George seen by Arthur Morcom. In Jack's hands George's leadership crumbles; his intellectual lead cannot help him; he is the subordinate partner who acquiesces in shady deals which, left to himself, would be unthinkable to him. To Lewis Eliot he retains to the end some vestige of the old gleam. In Arthur Morcom's eyes he is simply a foolish man with some charisma but no judgement. Another example of Snow's relative perception of character is hinted at in *The Light and the Dark* where, despite his unalterable endowment of black despair, Roy Calvert hopes that marriage to Rosalind will lighten his burden simply because Rosalind does not know what a spiritual crisis is. With her he changes a little, seems to himself more normal, tends to become, in fact, what she perceives him to be. For the same reason, Joan Royce, who fully understands him, has to be rejected. Eliot too is fended off by Roy because he understands too much. After marrying Rosalind, he is beginning to move towards hope when he dies. This delicate question of perception and changes of character that accompany it are fascinatingly raised by Snow, but not enlarged upon, which, considering the large amount of analytical comment that he provides, is somewhat surprising. Pursued a little further it could have raised questions of a philosophical order about truth.

STYLE

Perhaps the feature of Snow's work which has aroused the most scathing criticism is his style. The critics cannot forgive him for not being instinctively alive to the richness and density of words, but writing instead in a fashion so apparently colourless and drab that it seems unexciting. I hope in the following pages to establish that Snow's manner of writing has been deliberately cultivated to suit a particular mood in history and aims at a special kind of effect. I shall also discuss his use of language and imagery.

The prevailing tone of Snow's fiction is characteristic of the unheroic temper of the times. This temper is allied with the rational, positivistic philosophy of Wittgenstein and G. E. Moore, both of whom have underlined the need for clarity in thought:

Everything that can be thought can be thought clearly. Everything that can be said can be said clearly.[35]

After the Second World War a reaction set in against romanticism and the ineffable, and writers turned to external realities and the ordinariness of life. In this spirit, Kingsley Amis, in the fifties, asked that we should not have any more poems on the grand themes for a few years, and Philip Larkin, in a poem called 'Born Yesterday' for Amis's daughter Sally, deliberately avoided the Yeatsian prayer and wished her 'nothing uncustomary' and 'an average of talent'. Understatement became a matter not of expression only; rather, it was a recognition of the value of the muted, the subdued, the reasonable and the unecstatic.

As G. S. Fraser has pointed out, this reaction almost certainly had something to do with the war, after which Europe, having had a daily surfeit of emotion, emerged in 1945 in a state of exhaustion and near-collapse. Young writers had seen too much of cruelty and elation to go in for intense responses for some time at least. Having been through disasters in which the existence of traditional institutions had been threatened, they felt a renewed respect for the decencies of ordinary, civilised life. There was, after this, no simple ideology which could satisfy them again as Marxism or the liberal faith had satisfied them in the thirties. One possible attitude was to be receptive and open and tolerant of all sorts of differences, and to preserve a balance between too presumptuous hope and too much despair. This attitude in turn led to writing which was low-keyed, only hinting at the emotional heights and hoping for a future without horrors. In literary technique the new mood led back to the realistic method and the solidities of the external scene became once more important. Ecstasy was almost suspect, furniture and bodies returned, and the density provided by the social scene once again began to fill out the novel. Snow's writing had been tuned to this mood long before it actually overtook Britain.

His first serious novel, *The Search,* was published in 1934 and the first volume of the *Strangers and Brothers* series came out in 1940. When they first appeared, with their analytical, understated, unheroic emphasis, both must have sounded oddly out of tune.

But Snow had his ear close to the ground and what he heard turned out to be right. It suited his temperament as a writer. In Snow's novel *Corridors of Power* Roger Quaife, making the most crucial speech of his political life, throws away rhetoric and speaks as plainly and simply as he can. Snow implies that rationalism and plain speaking are closely related; it is partly through his style (much-maligned) that Snow captures the mood of these last five decades.

There are three points about Snow's style which need to be established straight away. The first is that Snow does not seem to have started as a literary type with a born flair for writing. The second is that he is very deliberate and self-conscious in his use of language. The third point is that his writing has shown a marked increase of confidence, as if he feels now that he is perfecting his idiom and what the 'Eng. Lit.' types say does not matter a bit. I shall consider these points one by one.

It is common knowledge that Snow started out in life as a scientist.

Now, some scientists are very highly cultivated and fully aware of the power of language. Bronowski is an outstanding example of that combination. For Snow, development of a taste for literature must have been, I feel, a slower and less instinctive growth. Somewhere at the bottom he knew he always wanted to write, but both circumstance and endowments led him in another direction, and he returned to what he really wanted to do somewhat late. In any case, the spontaneous reaction of the literary type, however untutored, to the music of words was evidently not part of his sensibility. That reaction is summed up by Dylan Thomas in an early letter to Pamela Hansford Johnson:

> There must be no compromise; there is always one right word; use it.
> . . . It is part of a poet's job to take a debauched and prostituted word,
> like the beautiful word 'blond,' and to smooth away the lines of its
> dissipation, and to put it on the market again, fresh and virginal.[36]

Words by themselves could not, I feel, have excited Snow in this manner. In short, his is not a poetic temperament though he has trained himself to understand the poetic sensibility. In an article in the *Kenyon Review* Snow suggests that translations into another language lose little if the intention of the writer is large enough; and that it is absurd to regard a work of art as a structure of words which is irreducible.[37] One might note that the important acknowledged influences on himself (Tolstoy, Dostoevsky, Balzac, Proust) are writers whom he may have read in translation. The stress on science in his formative school years must have meant less time for reading literature. One gathers that he read a great deal but not especially the English classics. He has said in an interview that he was forty years old before he really started reading Dickens in a serious and thorough way.[38] Possibly, when he read *A Tale of Two Cities* he was more fascinated by the character of Sydney Carton, so beautifully underdone, than by the rhythms of the famous opening. What this has resulted in is the most *un-allusive* style that I can think of amongst English novelists. He is the very opposite of Anthony Powell who, when he sees a workman at a street corner, is reminded by his nose of a Shakespearean clown,[39] and whose prose is laced with deliberate allusions to painting. In the case of Snow the rare allusion to Yeats or Shakespeare comes as a surprise because it is so untypical. It is worth noting that whatever allusions there are occur in the much later novels – that is, after years of schooling himself, he slips them in unobtrusively. In *Last Things* Lewis Eliot refers to himself as 'an aging public man' and uses the phrase 'who's in, who's out'. The phrase 'cast a cold eye' occurs in *In Their Wisdom*. These are among the few exceptions.

The lack of allusions admittedly deprives the style of richness and makes it bare, in a sense naked. But there is also some gain. The unallusiveness gives an impression of transparency and freshness, a sense of honesty and, yes, originality. T. S. Eliot in modern times has shown us the splendour of allusion; the line in 'The Wasteland', for instance, from Spenser's 'Prothalamion', placed in the midst of modern decay is daring and original to the highest degree. But we have become so much accustomed to such literary tradition that the spareness of Snow's style comes as something new and touching.

Apart from the early absence of the literary background, his scientific training may have positively affected Snow's style of writing – a style that has been called the Royal Society style. In 1667 Thomas Sprat, writing a history of the Royal Society, attacked rhetorical and figurative language; its members had rejected all amplifications, digressions and swellings of style.

> They have exacted from all their members a close, naked, natural way of speaking; positive expressions; clear senses; a native easiness; bringing all things as near the Mathematical plainness, as they can; and preferring the language of Artizans, Countrymen and Merchants before that of Wits, or Scholars.[40]

The simplicity described in the foregoing paragraph shows us the tradition of writing which may well have influenced Snow and made him prefer the penny plain over the tuppence coloured. He chooses always the undecorative word. In his biography of Trollope he notes approvingly how Tolstoy aimed at the simplest possible style. Of Tolstoy Snow says:

> . . . time and time again he deletes a picturesque word and repeats one already used. It was one of the most thorough revisions in history. Though it has struck some critics as monstrous, yet for his purpose, the purpose of ultimate directness, it was of course right. When he indulged himself he was one of the most eloquent of writers. . . . In dealing with his characters he wasn't indulging himself. He was cutting out everything except telling the truth.[41]

This is very close to Snow's feeling about his own style. In a letter to me he says that he does prefer the plain over the decorative word, and in the REL interview he admits that his typical manuscript is full of revisions, saying 'It is a very messy crossed-out kind of manuscript'.[42]

Quite clearly then Snow's plain style is deliberately and self-consciously adopted. The Light and the Dark proves to us that Snow is capable of writing an emotive prose quite different from the one we usually associate with him. Evidently Snow has hammered out his later style carefully as expressive of his view of truth. Some critics have felt that it is banal and indefensible; that Snow, as Wyndham Lewis said of Orwell, is 'jotting down the first jolly old word that came into his jolly old head'.[43] True, there is none of the precious poring over words or the daring reinvigoration of them advised by Dylan Thomas. But Snow's prose impresses one as the result of a careful search for the right tone and word to express a particular way of apprehending things, the best way of communicating the ordinariness, the countless, unnoticed moments of life as lived from day to day in a society highly utilitarian and materialistic. For the evocation of the unheightened moments and the daily texture of experience Snow's style is very well suited. The most characteristic Snowian sentence rarely draws attention to itself. Here is a typical example from *Homecomings*.

> He was so little stiff that Rose felt his own stiffness soften, and enjoyed the sensation: sometimes his refusal to stay at a distance, his zest for breathing down one's neck, made him paradoxically welcome to correct and buttoned natures.[44]

This cool, flattish tone is the prevailing one in most of the novels. The style grows on one till one begins to understand how successful it is in re-creating a particular tone of voice and particular way of responding.

Bernard Bergonzi in *The Situation of the Novel* has an interesting chapter called 'The Ideology of Being English' in which he contrasts the drab and mechanical non-style of the average English novel with the inflated over-writing of the average American novel. Both, of course, are bad, but at least the Americans try hard; some energy is expended on the conscious use of words. At a superficial glance, Snow would seem to fall into the class of the anonymous non-style writers. A second perusal shows that nothing could be further from the truth.

Understatement, playing things down, has become a national characteristic of the English, and it is this mode of thought and expression that Snow consistently uses. Pamela Hansford Johnson in a very interesting article called 'Modern Fiction and English Understatement' in the *TLS* some years ago makes two points. The first is that understatement, even while it has denuded the novel, can be a good thing because it is a barrier against cruelty and callousness and does far less harm than overstatement is likely to do. Her second point is that too much understatement can be moral danger. Giving an example she says

> Referring to bombs as 'hardware' tends to anaesthetise the public mind against the realisation of what those bombs do to human flesh.[45]

Here she is restating George Orwell's main point in his essay 'Politics and the English Language', where he protests against the use of jargon which blinds the human mind to the horrible fact. The conviction that understatement is a barrier against cruelty seems to me to underlie Snow's style. Given his accepting cast of mind, he resorts naturally to this device: overstatement involves stronger emphasis and more rigorous exclusion than Snow is prepared to bring to any consideration of life. Snow also adopts an absolutely simple, jargon-free language to describe the horror of atomic warfare.[46]

On the whole Snow uses understatement with fine effect as, for example, when he tells us that the dying Master was often absent-minded, 'as though he were trying to become familiar with his fate'.[47] Or when he gives Roger Quaife's crucial speech on disarmament from which it is clear that Snow recognises that the low-keyed tone is the contemporary tone. Lewis Eliot remarks about Quaife's speech:

> As he got down to the arguments, he was using the idiom of a late twentieth-century man. He had thrown away the old style of parliamentary rhetoric altogether. Compared with the other speeches from both the front benches, this might have come from a man a generation younger. It was the speech of one used to broadcasting studios, television cameras, the exposure of the machine. He didn't declaim: he spoke about war, weapons, the meaning of a peaceful future, in his own voice. This was how, observers said later, parliamentarians would be speaking in ten years time.[48]

It is interesting to see that there is in Snow a lyrical bent which is deliberately suppressed. The only novel in which this strain comes uppermost is *The Light and the Dark,* which Peter Fison calls his 'farewell to youth'.[49] Here, the words and rhythms are in tune with the intense emotion at the heart of the book and the prose has cadences one never hears again. I quote below Eliot's thoughts about his friend Roy Calvert:

> But I knew that I should have wished him more commonplace and selfish, if only he could cease to be so haunted.
> Since I was close to him, I could see that little distance. But he exhilarated me with his gaiety, pierced me with his selflessness, deepened all I knew of life, gave my spirit wings: so I too did not see much that fate had done to him and I hoped that he would be happy.[50]

The whole book is in this vein, though Snow has generally toned it down for the final three-volume edition. It gives convincing proof that Snow is not always and entirely the cold, rational, factual writer but is aware of rhetorical device and the value of pause and rhythm in the evocation of feeling.

The most evocative moments in Snow's prose are often descriptions of the urban scene, the town by night, the city sometimes derelict but always haunted. For instance:

> ... to quieten my nerves, I spent the middle of the afternoon walking in the town, looking at bookshops, greeting acquaintances; the streets were busy, the window lights shone under the dark sky. There was the wishful smell of the Cambridge autumn, and in the tailor's shops gleamed the little handbills, blue letters on white with the names of the week's university teams.[51]

Or again, at the end of *Corridors of Power,* the darkened sky over London and the lives of those on the streets below:

> Over the garden, over the rooftops, shone the rusty, vivid night-sky of London, the diffused recognition of all those lives. . . . Under the town's resplendent sky we talked of the children and their future. We talked as though the future were easy and secure, and as though their lives would bring us joy.[52]

Occasionally, there is also a somewhat unexpected streak in the writing, a sort of yearning or wishfulness, that breaks out now and again. In different places in *The Affair* Eliot is touched by a feeling he cannot fully articulate, something mixed up with the landscape outside the comfortable room. I quote an instance:

> Outside the conference room windows it was a piercing blue April afternoon, a sunny afternoon with a wind so cold and pure that it made one catch one's breath. As we sat there in the Old Schools, I looked out at the bright light, resentful at being kept in, resentful without understanding why, as though the strings of memory were being plucked, as though once I had been out in the cold free air and known great happiness. And yet, my real memories of days like that in Cambridge were sad ones.[53]

Last Things, the final volume of the *Strangers and Brothers* sequence, has few touches of the earlier youthful emotion. The accounts of the operation and survival are written in the flattest prose. There is nothing at all to make it more acceptable, no high moments of feeling; what emerges is resentment, even peevishness; and it seems surprisingly right. But it has some evocative touches, as for instance when young Charles Eliot is seen walking home in a blessed haze after his first sexual experience:

> 'Good God,' said Gordon, pointing up the street towards Marble Arch. There was a solitary figure on the pavement, sauntering very slowly. When it passed into zones illuminated by the arc lamps, one saw it through lances of rain.[54]

In an article on Svevo the Italian writer, Snow describes Trieste, the setting for Svevo's novels. I quote a line to show how Snow, though he may write for the most part in a deliberately bald fashion, is fully capable of using nuances of style, rhythm and rhetorical devices, the most obvious of which, after *The Light and the Dark,* he usually avoids. He writes about Trieste:

> Everything that Svevo wrote is set there, and the beautiful city, beautiful as Quebec is beautiful, not so much because of the buildings in detail, but because of the shape of the streets, the colours, the light and water, looks down on Svevo's old men, his young optimistic bumblers, the affectionate girls.[55]

The rise and fall of that sentence, with its qualifying clauses, the repetition of beautiful, the omission of 'and' before the phrase 'the affectionate girls' – all combine to communicate the emotion of the writer as he contemplates both Trieste and Svevo.

In an early novel there are some remarks about sensitivity to words which indicate that Snow is certainly not as naïve about this aspect of the novelist's craft as some critics have supposed. Lewis Eliot, visiting his friend in Germany, finds himself cut off by the fog of a foreign language:

> Both he and I picked up so much from words and from the feeling behind words. He could tell from the form of a sentence, from the hesitation over a word, some new event in the librarian's life.[56]

Interestingly, Lewis Eliot comments on his own change in styles. Recalling earlier days when he had used the antique Japanese phrase for obsessive love, 'darkness of the heart', he remarks, 'Nowadays the phrase had become too florid for my taste'.[57] Elsewhere he speaks of the 'dry, analytic language of the day'.[58]

Snow, then, certainly understands the resources of the language though he does not choose to use many of them; and he does not 'just write' in a mechanical and anonymous way but has given thought to the problem of the style best suited to his purpose. For one who does not attempt to cast on the world about him the light that never was on sea or land his style works admirably, revealing the presence of a subdued imagination brooding over the whole sequence. Jack Story in an engaging review of *In Their Wisdom* in *The Listener,* uses a line from that novel when he says that reading too much Snow is like being beaten over the head with a very soft pillow.[59] He has his tongue firmly tucked in his cheek, of course, but he may be saying that there is something definable about Snow's style. It is *not* a non-style. There is an evenness about it and a lack of sensuous detail that tend to depress, but every now and then, he will give us flashes which strike us not only because they are full of insight but because of their rightness of phrasing.

Having made these points about the deliberate and conscious nature of Snow's style I must admit that the weaknesses are striking and that when the writing is bad it is horrid. It can sound uninspired and monotonous and it can fall into bathos. Snow is capable of writing a clause like 'each heart-beat served him and him alone'. But the important thing is that such lapses do not occur very often. Usually the choice of words seems right for the events and people being described, and it is very largely through the style, itself an outcome of a reasonable and reasoning temperament, that Lewis Eliot's sensibility is gradually borne in upon us. Brady notes that Snow's direct and laconic style has a beauty of its own – 'the beauty, say, of a Flemish plain'.[60]

Rayner Heppenstall has great fun mocking some of Snow's unhappier phrases: 'feeling things in the fibres' for instance, or of 'having' Margaret in a sexual sense (not at all becoming in civil servants, says Heppenstall, really a gangster expression!).[61] Heppenstall also remarks that some phrases are positively obscure. As an example, he picks a line about Sir Hector Rose: 'he had permitted himself that last arctic flick'.[62] What can it mean, he wonders? It may be an odd phrase but it obviously means a sarcastic rejoinder; and the use of 'flick' brings out very nicely the elegant and cool manner, the gesture of the shrugged shoulder almost, or better, the raised eyebrow.

The third and last point about Snow's use of language is its gradual development. Since the publication of *Variety of Men* there is discernible in his style a growing self-assurance and command. He has got over the laborious part and the writing flows with much greater ease. It is as plain as ever but it pours out with extreme confidence. In a novel of the middle period, in *The New Men* for example, the style limps along somewhat, determined to be undecorated but not very sure of itself. There are too many flat paragraphs strung together without the sub-dued emotion which flows like a current below the surface of many of the other novels. By contrast, by the time we come to *In Their Wisdom,* the writer is very definitely the master of his content and style. He can throw off a clause like 'he was unqualmish about his own mortality' without a blink. About an unpleasant doctor he writes:

> And Pemberton, who not only despised vigorously but was good at contempt, had considerable contempt for those who indulged themselves in drawing-room emotions. What did it matter who one's heir was? What did they matter, most of the emotions people wrote books about? If you had been a doctor and lived your life in the presence of the primary emotions, then the rest of people's worries and hopes were trivial – bits of playing, luxuries you could afford because you had nothing serious on your mind.[63]

This passage, with its questions and answer, its plain words and the robust movement of its phrases, quite successfully conveys Pemberton's flexing of his mental muscles, his irritability and practicality. In the same novel the same plain style is used to communicate a sense of something far different – impending death. In an excellent scene with Lord Hillmorton, who is dying of cancer, and Sedgwick, who has Parkinson's disease, the writer tells us that Sedgwick, visiting Hillmorton, 'felt better, sinfully better, warm with relief . . . like someone who had been dragged from a car crash, knowing that his companions were still inside'. After a few slow exchanges, Hillmorton says: 'It does seem rather strange, don't you know'. And the author comments finely:

> What? Coming towards death in this tidy, suburban bed-room? Just dying? It had been said with an edge of incredulity, without fuss.[64]

That is a beautiful and quiet handling of horror realised, as effective in its way as Graham Greene's more heightened style, from which I quote below:

> He put his hands on the dressing table and held to it; he said to himself over and over again, 'I must stand up, I must stand up,' as though there were some virtue in simply remaining on his feet while his brain reeled with the horror of returning life.[65]

To quote snippets from *In Their Wisdom* is not a very good thing to do for the triumph of the book is in the whole; fine passages do not stand out; every chapter and paragraph is as good as the one before or after. It is amazing to see how Snow has picked himself up after *The Malcontents*; and attained in his latest novel a new sense of workmanship and attention to craft and detail.

One striking fact about Snow's style is that deliberately he keeps it as close to the spoken idiom as possible. Even in the long passages of analysis and reflection it does not become any more formal or removed from colloquial speech. It is an indication of the very keen ear he has for the rhythms and phrases of the spoken language. As a result he sounds always direct and without artifice, though plainly it must take a good deal of artifice to sound so consistently natural. He has admitted that he finds writing a slow and exhausting process.

Perhaps the most marked feature of Snow's style, next to its plainness, is the relative absence of complex imagery and metaphor. Alistair Macdonald has made a study of the imagery in Snow's novels[66] but this seems to me to be misdirected. To compare, as he does, Snow's image-world to Webster's and to refer to his 'metaphysical yoking together' of cliché and non-cliché phrases gives entirely the wong emphasis to his style. Snow's imagination is as far removed from Webster's as it is possible to be.

In the previous chapter I have ventured to suggest that he may have tentatively used George Passant and Adam Sedgwick as symbols of two important movements of our time. However, by and large, Snow does not usually resort to symbolism and, as is evident from remarks of his quoted in Chapter 1 of this book, is not really comfortable with it. Imagery, too, is used very sparingly. Anthony Burgess complains of the lack of sensuous detail in Snow's writing, associating him with Dr Johnson's Imlac because he spends all his remarks on general properties and large appearances, and does not number the strokes of the tulip or describe the different shades in the verdure of the forest.[67] Such a lack leads to denudation doubtless, a colourlessness above everything else. The world is seen consistently in shades of grey, and obviously the sensuous response does not come very readily to Snow.

Of course he has his own set of favourite images which are all the more noticeable because they occur rarely. The oblique effect of metaphor has been ruthlessly excluded because the writer wishes to communicate usually at the literal, factual level, and metaphor inevitably evokes associations wider than itself and hints at a richness of feeling that Snow usually does not wish to suggest. He has chosen austerity and dryness to express his insight; he is totally different from his contemporary (and, judging from the dedication of *Nothing Like the Sun*, also his friend), Anthony Burgess, whose every line evokes a host of associations and whose language streams out from an extraordinary fecund source, recalling the dazzling verbal imagery of Joyce. The fact is that most writers have that ability to greater and lesser degrees. A fluency which is not based on a wealth of images within but is still sensitive to sound and rhythm is rarer. What it arises from, I believe, is the dominance of Snow's auditory sense over his visual. This is why there is so little *colour* in his novels; the prevailing colour is grey. And when, in the middle of his dry, spare writing he breaks out with an image or two – the city by night, lights streaming along the river, for instance, or 'the sprinkle of rain, the settled dust',[68] – then the unexpected, toned-down image strikes us with delicacy and freshness.

A recurring image is that of the warm, comfortably-lit room curtained off from the cold outside. Bergonzi has interestingly interpreted this 'warm-room fire-blazing' image as expressive of a Freudian wish to return to the womb.[69] Certainly it is a recurring motif, with Lewis Eliot sometimes looking on wistfully from the outside, sometimes securely within. I believe that this image recurs so frequently because Snow has a deep-seated feeling about a manageable and snug environment with its promise of order and comfort. The larger society, too, with which he deals, is one on which the reason seeks to impose order, make civilised – the abstract equivalents of the warmth and snugness. The homecoming to the pleasant, well-lit house (at the end of *Homecomings*) is really what Snow wants for everyone, everywhere. Reason should prevail so that safety and order are assured. I think one should recognise that this is not just crass materialism but an instinct for the civilised and harmonious graces of life, an instinct not unlike that of the Augustans of the eighteenth century. It may seem limited as theirs seemed limited to the fervent Romantics, but it is expressive of stability, both mental and social. Definitely a product of education, Snow's mind is of the sort that would find terror and unreason totally alien and repelling. I do not believe this contradicts Bergonzi's Freudian interpretation; but the warm-room image, arising out of a preoccupation with order, reason and security, may have emerged also from the slightly more conscious levels of the creating mind.

To sum up: Snow's style is quite deliberately plain. He has an excellent ear for contemporary idiom and tricks of speech. He resorts constantly to understatement. As a rule, he consciously eschews symbol and metaphor and clearly he has no great store of them. He has a romantic yearning usually held firmly in check, a lyrical bent deliberately suppressed. But it is a thin sort of emotion leading to a corresponding thinness of texture which has its own austere appeal. One is reminded of Arnold's poetry and the touching greyness which pervades it. Perhaps the cultivation of the reason or over-education contributes to the toned-down, colourless habit. Perhaps it is a cultivated feeling that excess simply is not 'good form'. But more likely it rises from a temperament that yearns (how much there is of that in Arnold's poetry) but whose senses seldom ache. For all the striking differences of opinion and taste, somewhere at the source of their sensual natures, Snow and Arnold seem to me to be similar.

Notes

CHAPTER 1

1 Following Stephen Spender's broad terms in *The Struggle of the Modern* (Berkeley: University of California Press, 1963).

2 C. P. Snow, *In Their Wisdom* (New York: Scribner, 1974) p. 345.

3 C. P. Snow, *The Sleep of Reason* (London: Penguin, 1971) p. 232.

4 C. P. Snow, *The Masters* (London: Penguin, 1969) p. 283.

5 Helen Gardner, 'The World of C. P. Snow', *New Statesman*, 55 (1958) 409.

6 Angus Wilson, 'Diversity and Depth', *TLS*, 15 Aug 1958, p. viii.

7 L. P. Hartley, 'The Novelist and his Material', *TLS*, 15 Aug 1958, p. iv.

8 C. P. Snow, 'Trollope: The Psychological Stream', in *On the Novel*, ed. B. S. Benedikz (London: Dent, 1971) p. 12.

9 C. P. Snow, 'Challenge to the Intellect', *TLS*, 15 Aug 1958, p. iii.

10 'Experience of a Lifetime', *TLS*, 20 June 1958, p. 345.

11 'Interview with C. P. Snow', *Review of English Literature*, 3 (1962) 93.

12 Rubin Rabinovitz, *The Reaction Against the Experimental Novel* (New York: Columbia University Press, 1967) p. 152.

13 C. P. Snow, *The Affair* (London: Penguin, 1970) p. 103.

14 C. P. Snow, *Corridors of Power* (London: Penguin, 1972) p. 103.

15 Pamela Hansford Johnson [Lady Snow], *Important to Me* (New York: Scribner, 1974) p. 174.

16 Johnson, *Important to Me*, p. 32.

17 Johnson, *Important to Me*, p. 217. The eye-patch is clearly visible in a photograph of Lord Snow as Rector of St Andrews University reproduced in R. Greacen, *The World of C. P. Snow* (London, 1963).

18 Johnson, *Important to Me*, p. 32.

19 C. P. Snow, *Variety of Men* (New York: Scribner, 1967) p. 22, and *Homecomings* (London: Penguin, 1966) p. 203.

20 *Variety*, p. 54, and *Homecomings*, p. 205.

21 *Variety*, p. 59.

22 In a letter to me Snow says that some of his own beliefs about novel-writing are inevitably implicit in his biography of Trollope.

23 C. P. Snow, *Trollope: His Life and Art* (New York: Scribner, 1975) p. 62.

24 Frank Kermode, 'The House of Fiction: Interviews with Seven English

Novelists', *Partisan Review*, 30 (1963) 75.

25 Raymond Williams, 'Realism and the Contemporary Novel', *Partisan Review*, 26 (1959) 205.

26 Kermode, 'House of Fiction', p. 74.

27 Bernard Bergonzi, *The Situation of the Novel* (London: Pelican, 1972) p. 162.

28 Pamela Hansford Johnson, 'Debate About the Novel', *New Statesman*, 56 (9 Aug 1958) 172.

29 'Experience of a Lifetime', *TLS*, p. 345.

30 Richard Lehan, '*The Masters* Examined' in *Six Contemporary Novels*, ed. W. O. S. Sutherland (Austin: University of Texas Press, 1962), p. 57.

31 William F. Hall, 'The Humanism of C. P. Snow', *Wisconsin Studies in Contemporary Literature*, 4 (1963) 205.

32 Rabinovitz, *Reaction*, p. 149.

33 Quoted by Bergonzi, *Situation*, p. 123.

34 Derek Stanford, 'C. P. Snow: The Novelist as Fox', *Meanjin*, 19 (1960) 241.

35 Bernard Bergonzi, 'The World of Lewis Eliot', *Twentieth Century*, 67 (1960) 219.

36 Richard Lehan comments on Eliot's 'superhuman insight' in '*The Masters* Examined', p. 55.

37 C. P. Snow, *The Light and the Dark* (New York: Scribner, 1947) p. 184.

38 R. A. Solokov, 'Strangers and Brothers', *Newsweek*, 17 Aug 1970, p. 88.

CHAPTER 2

 1 'Interview with C. P. Snow', *Review of English Literature*, 3 (July 1962) 105.

 2 C. P. Snow, *The Light and the Dark* (New York: Scribner, 1947) p. 13.

 3 C. P. Snow, *The Sleep of Reason* (London: Penguin, 1971) p. 186.

 4 C. P. Snow, *Homecomings* (London: Penguin, 1966), p. 227.

 5 *Homecomings*, p. 227.

 6 C. P. Snow, *The Affair* (London: Penguin, 1970) p. 121.

 7 Kathleen Nott, 'The Type to which the whole creation moves: thoughts on the Snow saga,' *Encounter*, 18 (1962) 96.

 8 *The Affair*, p. 137.

 9 C. P. Snow, *Last Things* (London: Macmillan, 1970) p. 41.

10 *The Affair*, p. 38.

11 C. P. Snow, *In Their Wisdom* (New York: Scribner, 1974) p. 23.

12 *Homecomings*, p. 258.

13 'Of Bureaucratic Man', *Times Literary Supplement*, 7 May 1954, p. 296.

14 C. P. Snow, *Strangers and Brothers* (London: Penguin, 1962) p. 314.

15 Helen Gardner, 'The World of C. P. Snow', *New Statesman*, 55 (1958) 409.

16 The *TLS* review of the book (though unsigned, it was surely written by Rayner Heppenstall since much of it reappears in his *The Fourfold Tradition*) observes: 'Snow would not do very well in an examination of Jewish thought and custom. The Marches are not essentially different from the Forsytes.' *Times Literary Supplement*, 28 Mar 1958, p. 165.

17 *The Light and the Dark*, p. 304.

18 Derek Stanford, 'The Novelist as Fox,' *Meanjin*, 19 (1960) 251.

19 C. P. Snow, *The New Men* (London: Penguin, 1970) p. 143.

20 *Homecomings*, p. 213.

21 Sidney Pollard, 'History: Economic and Social' in *The Twentieth Century*

Mind, ed. C. B. Cox and A. E. Dyson (London: Oxford Paperbacks, 1972)
p. 31.

22 Pollard, p. 32.

23 *The Affair*, p. 23.

24 C. P. Snow, *Corridors of Power* (London: Penguin, 1972) p. 19.

25 *Corridors*, p. 269.

26 *Corridors*, p. 110.

27 *London Magazine*, 4 (1964) 102.

28 See Pamela Hansford Johnson, *On Iniquity: some personal reflections arising out of the Moors Murder trials* (London: Macmillan, 1967).

29 When a man is caught in homosexual soliciting, the general comment is, 'That chap had hard luck.' (*Corridors*, p. 83).

30 In *Last Things* Eliot remarks: 'The irony was, that the freedom George – and all the other Georges of his time – had clamoured for, had more or less come true. The life that Charles's own friends were leading was not that much different from what George had foreshadowed all those years ago. A lot of the young men and girls in the Earl's Court bedsitter would have fitted . . . into George's group. Gentle. Taking their pleasures as they came. Not liking their society any more than George had done. Making their own enclaves. . . . The same belief, deep down, that most people were good'. *Last Things*, p. 79.

31 *The Sleep of Reason*, p. 221.

32 *Corridors*, p. 284.

33 Lionel Trilling, 'The Novel Alive or Dead', *A Gathering of Fugitives* (Boston: Beacon Press, 1956) p. 120.

34 David Lodge, 'The Contemporary Novel and all that Jazz', *London Magazine*, 2 (Aug 1962) 76.

35 'Diversity and Depth', *TLS*, 15 Aug 1958.

36 'What is a novel?', *TLS*, 9 May 1958.

CHAPTER 3

1 Helen Gardner, 'The World of C. P. Snow', *New Statesman*, 55 (1958) 410.

2 C. P. Snow, *Time of Hope* (London: Penguin, 1962) p. 327.

3 'Interview with C. P. Snow', *Review of English Literature*, 3 (July 1962) 107.

4 This impression has been deliberately toned down in the revised three volume edition of *Strangers and Brothers* (New York: Scribner, 1972).

5 C. P. Snow, *The Light and the Dark* (New York: Scribner, 1974) p. 145.

6 *The Light and the Dark*, p. 75.

7 D. H. Lawrence's phrase quoted by Frank Kermode, 'Beckett, Snow and Pure Poverty', *Encounter*, 15 (July 1960) 76.

8 C. P. Snow, *In Their Wisdom* (New York: Scribner, 1974) p. 53.

9 Bernard Bergonzi, *The Situation of the Novel* (London: Pelican, 1972) p. 168.

10 E. W. Mandel, 'C. P. Snow's Fantasy of Politics', *Queen's Quarterly*, 69 (1962) 24 ff.

11 K. Hamilton, 'C. P. Snow and Political Man', *Queen's Quarterly*, 69 (1962) 416ff.

12 *The Light and the Dark*, p. 287.

13 *The Light and the Dark*, p. 383.

14 C. P. Snow, *The Search* (London: Penguin, 1965) pp. 262–5.
15 *The Search*, p. 270.
16 *The Search*, p. 318.
17 C. P. Snow, *The Conscience of the Rich* (London: Penguin, 1966) p. 73.
18 *The Conscience of the Rich*, p. 305.
19 Ibid.
20 Ibid.
21 C. P. Snow, *Time of Hope* (London: Penguin, 1962) p. 358.
22 C. P. Snow, *Variety of Men* (New York: Scribner, 1967) p. 108.
23 C. P. Snow, *Homecomings* (London: Penguin, 1966) p. 238.
24 Rayner Heppenstall, *The Fourfold Tradition* (London: Barrie, 1961) p. 234.
25 R. Rabinovitz, *The Reaction Against Experiment in the English Novel: 1950–1960* (New York: Columbia University Press, 1967) p. 164.
26 Rabinovitz, *Reaction*, p. 164.
27 *Homecomings*, p. 84.
28 Rabinovitz. *Reaction*, p. 158.
29 *Homecomings*, p. 152.
30 C. P. Snow, *Strangers and Brothers*, now re-titled *George Passant* (London: Penguin, 1962) p. 115.
31 Towards the end of the series Martineau is mentioned as a pavement artist in the streets of London and in *Last Things* we hear that he has given up his wayfaring life, married a good woman and now, in his sixties, plays happily with his infant children.
32 *The Light and the Dark*, p. 77.
33 C. P. Snow, *The New Men* (London: Penguin, 1970) p. 151.
34 *The New Men*, p. 210.
35 *The New Men*, p. 228.
36 Rabinovitz, *Reaction*, p. 161.
37 C. P. Snow, *Corridors of Power* (London: Penguin, 1972) p. 334.
38 In contrast, Leverett-Smith, who later becomes Secretary when Quaife is Minister, supports him in his crisis. See *Corridors*, p. 300.
39 *Corridors*, p. 208.
40 *Corridors*, p. 211.
41 *Corridors*, p. 271.
42 *Corridors*, p. 271.
43 *Listener*, 20 Feb 1975, p. 240.
44 'The Novelist's World', *Times Literary Supplement*, 6 Sep 1957, p. 533.

CHAPTER 4

1 E. W. Mandel, 'C. P. Snow's Fantasy of Politics,' *Queen's Quarterly*, 69 (1962) 24.
2 C. P. Snow, *The Masters* (London: Penguin, 1969), p. 264.
3 C. P. Snow, 'In the Communities of the Elite,' *TLS*, 15 Oct 1971, p. 1249.
4 As a generalisation this may not stand up very well. The two tramps in Beckett's *Waiting for Godot* belong to no elite; there are no contrasts, no free personality, nothing. Yet they are as exciting to the existential imagination as Snow's privileged group is to the realist. And why should a privileged character be freer in personality than any other except in the sense that knowledge brings suffering or education can enlarge the range of desire?

5 C. P. Snow, *Last Things* (London: Macmillan, 1970), p. 32.

6 Bernard Bergonzi has noted how frequently the word 'cosy' recurs in Snow's writing in an article, 'The World of Lewis Eliot', *Twentieth Century*, 167 (1960) 214.

7 An article entitled 'The Novelist's World' in the *TLS* warned the contemporary English novel against the 'danger of relaxing into the small humours of a grumbling, self-enclosed cosiness.' *TLS*, 6 Sep. 1957, p. 533.

8 *Last Things*, p. 31.

9 Richard Mayne, 'The Club Armchair', *Encounter*, 21 (1963) 76.

10 *The Masters*, p. 281.

11 C. P. Snow, *The Light and the Dark* (New York: Scribner, 1947) p. 346.

12 E. W. Mandel, 'C. P. Snow's Fantasy of Politics,' *Queen's Quarterly*, 69 (1962) 34. I am indebted to this article for its discussion of the individual versus the group.

13 *The Light and the Dark*, p. 24.

14 C. P. Snow, *Homecomings* (London: Penguin, 1966), p. 255.

15 Ibid.

16 *The Masters*, p. 94.

17 *The Masters*, p. 257.

18 *Homecomings*, p. 155.

19 *Homecomings*, p. 247.

20 *Homecomings*, p. 254.

21 *The Masters*, p. 273.

22 *The Masters*, p. 274.

23 *The Light and the Dark*, p. 345.

24 *The Light and the Dark*, p. 261.

25 *The Conscience of the Rich* (London: Penguin, 1966) p. 160.

26 'The Workaday World the Novelist Never Enters', *TLS*, 9 Sep. 1960, p. vii.

27 'The Making of an Idea', *TLS*, 15 Aug 1958.

CHAPTER 5

1 C. P. Snow, *In Their Wisdom* (New York: Scribner, 1974) p. 34.

2 *In Their Wisdom*, p. 160.

3 C. P. Snow, *The Sleep of Reason* (London: Penguin, 1971), p. 403.

4 *In Their Wisdom*, p. 161.

5 *In Their Wisdom*, p. 163.

6 *In Their Wisdom*, p. 164.

7 *In Their Wisdom*, p. 51.

8 *In Their Wisdom,* p. 53.

9 Ibid,

10 *In Their Wisdom*, p. 143.

11 *In Their Wisdom*, p. 53.

12 *In Their Wisdom*, p. 38.

13 *In Their Wisdom*, p. 58.

14 *In Their Wisdom*, p. 147.

15 *In Their Wisdom*, p. 144.

16 *In Their Wisdom*, p. 257.

17 *In Their Wisdom*, p. 331.

18 Patrick Swinden, 'The World of C. P. Snow', *Critical Quarterly*, 15 (winter 1973) 312.

19 C. P. Snow, *The Light and the Dark* (New York: Scribner, 1947), p. 87.
20 C. P. Snow, *The Light and the Dark*, p. 383.
21 C. P. Snow, *The Light and the Dark*, p. 182.
22 C. P. Snow, *The Light and the Dark*, p. 165. The Italics are mine.
23 C. P. Snow, *The Sleep of Reason*, p. 387.

CHAPTER 6

1 Edmund Fuller, *Books with Men Behind Them* (New York: Random House, 1962), p. 108.
2 Malcolm Bradbury, *Possibilities: Essays on the State of the Novel* (Oxford: OUP Paperbacks, 1974), p. 204.
3 Bernard Bergonzi, 'The World of Lewis Eliot', *Twentieth Century*, 167 (1960) 217.
4 Pamela Hansford Johnson, 'Three Novelists and the Drawing of Character: C. P. Snow, Joyce Cary and Ivy Compton-Burnett', *Essays and Studies* (London, 1950) p. 82.
5 C. P. Snow, *Strangers and Brothers*, now re-titled *George Passant* (London: Penguin, 1962) p. 310.
6 C. P. Snow, *Time of Hope* (London: Penguin, 1962), p. 247.
7 C. P. Snow, *Time of Hope*, p. 245.
8 'Interview with C. P. Snow,' *Review of English Literature*, 3 (July 1962) 99.
9 C. P. Snow, *In Their Wisdom* (New York: Scribner, 1974) p. 304.
10 *In Their Wisdom*, p. 325.
11 *In Their Wisdom*, p. 27.
12 *In Their Wisdom*, p. 151.
13 *In Their Wisdom*, p. 156.
14 C. P. Snow, *The Conscience of the Rich* (London: Penguin, 1966) p. 76.
15 *The Conscience of the Rich*, p. 123.
16 *The Conscience of the Rich*, p. 155.
17 *The Conscience of the Rich*, p. 217.
18 *The Conscience of the Rich*, p. 242.
19 C. P. Snow, *The Light and the Dark* (New York: Scribner, 1947) p. 91.
20 *The Light and the Dark*, p. 101.
21 *The Light and the Dark*, p. 177.
22 *The Light and the Dark*, p. 178.
23 *The Light and the Dark*, p. 180.
24 *The Light and the Dark*, p. 181.
25 *The Light and the Dark*, p. 187.
26 C. P. Snow, *Trollope: His Life and Art* (New York: Scribner, 1975) p. 155.
27 *The Light and the Dark*, p. 19.
28 *In Their Wisdom*, p. 273.
29 *In Their Wisdom*, p. 9.
30 Frederick Karl, *C. P. Snow: The Politics of Conscience* (Carbondale: Southern Illinois University Press, 1963).
31 Quoted by Charles Brady, 'The British Novel Today', *Thought*, 30 (1959–60) 537.
32 Charles Brady, 'British Novel', p. 537.
33 C. P. Snow, *The Affair* (London: Penguin, 1970), p. 144.

34 *In Their Wisdom*, pp. 7, 228, 246, 285.

35 Quoted by Derek Stanford, 'Report from London', *Western Review*, 21 (summer 1957) 293.

36 Quoted in a review of Dylan Thomas's letters in *TLS*, 2 Mar 1967.

37 C. P. Snow, 'Science, Politics and the Novelist', *Kenyon Review*, 23 (winter 1961) 1.

38 'Interview with C. P. Snow', *Review of English Literature*, 3 (July 1962) 104.

39 Anthony Powell, *A Question of Upbringing* in *A Dance to the Music of Time*, Vol. 1 (Boston: Little, Brown & Company, 1951) p. 1.

40 Quoted by C. L. Barber, *The Story of Language* (London: Pan Books, 1964) p. 211.

41 C. P. Snow, *Trollope*, p. 161.

42 'Interview', *REL*, p. 98.

43 Quoted by Geoffrey Wagner, 'Sociology and Fiction', *Twentieth Century*, 167 (Feb 1960) 110.

44 C. P. Snow, *Homecomings* (London: Penguin, 1966) p. 217.

45 Pamela Hansford Johnson, 'Modern Fiction and the English Under-statement', *TLS*, 7 Aug 1959, p. 111.

46 C. P. Snow, *The New Men* (London: Penguin, 1970) p. 154.

47 C. P. Snow, *The Light and the Dark*, p. 161.

48 C. P. Snow, *Corridors of Power* (London: Penguin, 1972) p. 332.

49 Peter Fison, 'A Reply to Benard Bergonzi's "World of Lewis Eliot" ', *Twentieth Century*, 167 (1960) 568.

50 *The Light and the Dark*, p. 42.

51 *The Light and the Dark*, p. 79.

52 *Corridors*, p. 352.

53 *The Affair*, p. 148.

54 C. P. Snow, *Last Things* (London: Macmillan, 1970) p. 221.

55 C. P. Snow, 'Svevo: Forerunner of Cooper and Amis', *Essays and Studies* (London, 1961) p. 15.

56 *The Light and the Dark*, p. 247.

57 C. P. Snow, *The Sleep of Reason* (London: Penguin, 1971) p. 89.

58 *The New Men*, p. 175.

59 Jack Story, 'Lid off the Lords', *Listener*, 10 Oct 1974, p. 482.

60 Brady, 'British Novel', p. 40.

61 Rayner Heppenstall, *The Fourfold Tradition* (London: Barrie, 1961) p. 236.

62 Heppenstall, p. 237.

63 *In Their Wisdom*, p. 80.

64 *In Their Wisdom*, p. 207.

65 Graham Greene, *The Ministry of Fear* (London: Penguin, 1965) p. 156.

66 A. Macdonald, 'Imagery in Snow', *University Review*, 33 (1966) 32.

67 Anthony Burgess, 'Powers That Be', *Encounter*, 24 (1965) 74.

68 *In Their Wisdom*, p. 138.

69 Bergonzi, 'World of Lewis Eliot,' p. 223.

Select Bibliography

The works listed below are the references used in the preparation of this book. They include a comprehensive bibliography of Snow's works and I have marked with an asterisk the editions I own and which were therefore most easily accessible to me. These are the editions for which page numbers are cited in the text although the three-volume omnibus collection of the eleven novels is now regarded as the definitive edition of the *Strangers and Brothers* sequence. The fullest bibliography of primary and secondary sources is to be found in R. Rabinovitz's *Reaction against Experiment in the English Novel* (New York: Columbia University Press, 1967).

Unsigned articles in *The Times Literary Supplement* and *Review of English Literature* appear under the names of the periodicals. Wherever the authorship is known articles appear under the authors listed alphabetically.

THE FICTION OF C. P. SNOW

Death Under Sail (London: Heinemann, 1932, 1959; Penguin, 1963, 1964).

The Search (London: Gollancz, 1934; Macmillan, 1958, 1959. New York: Scribner, 1959, 1969 paperback. Harmondsworth; Penguin, 1965*).

Strangers and Brothers (London: Faber and Faber, 1940; Macmillan, 1951, 1958. New York: Scribner, 1960, 1963 paperback. Harmondsworth: Penguin, 1962*).

The Light and the Dark (London: Faber and Faber, 1947; Macmillan, 1948, 1951, 1957. New York: Scribner, 1947*, 1961, 1964 paperback. Harmondsworth: Penguin, 1962, 1964).

Time of Hope (London: Faber and Faber, 1949; Macmillan, 1950, 1951, 1958. New York: Harper, 1961, paperback; Scribner, 1961, 1966 paperback. Harmondsworth: Penguin, 1962*).

The Masters (London, New York: Macmillan, 1951. New York: Scribner, 1951, 1960, 1965 paperback. London: Macmillan, 1954, 1959, 1972. Harmondsworth: Penguin, 1956*. Garden City, N.Y.: Doubleday, 1959 paperback).

The New Men (London, Toronto: Macmillan, 1954. New York: Scribner, 1955,

1961 paperback, 1965. London: Macmillan, 1958, 1960. Harmondsworth: Penguin, 1970*).

Homecomings (London: Macmillan, 1956. New York: Scribner, 1956, 1965 paperback. Harmondsworth: Penguin, 1966*).

The Conscience of the Rich (London: Macmillan, 1958 New York: Scribner, 1958, 1960 paperback. Harmondsworth: Penguin, 1966*).

The Affair (London: Macmillan, 1960. New York: Scribner, 1960. Harmondsworth: Penguin, 1962, 1970*).

Corridors of Power (London: Macmillan 1964. New York: Scribner, 1964; Bantam Books, 1965. Harmondsworth: Penguin, 1967, 1972*).

The Sleep of Reason (London: Macmillan, 1968. New York: Scribner, 1969. Harmondsworth: Penguin, 1970, 1971*).

Last Things (London: Macmillan, 1970.* New York: Scribner, 1970).

Strangers and Brothers Omnibus edn, three vols (London: Macmillan, 1972).

The Malcontents (London: Macmillan, 1972.* New York: Scribner, 1972).

In Their Wisdom (London: Macmillan, 1974. New York: Scribner, 1974*).

OTHER SELECTED WRITINGS OF C. P. SNOW

'New Minds for the New World', *New Statesman and Nation*, 52 (8.9.1956) 279–82. On scientific and technical education in Russia, the United States and Great Britain. Originally 'contributed by an expert who must necessarily remain anonymous' but subsequently identified by Snow as his.

'The English Realistic Novel', *Moderna Sprak*, 51(1957) 265–70.

'The Corridors of Power', *Listener*, 57(18.4.1957) 619–20.

'Changing Nature of Love', *Mademoiselle*, 46 (2.1958) 105, 180–1.

'Challenge to the Intellect', *The Times Literary Supplement*, 15.8.1958, p. iii.

The Two Cultures and the Scientific Revolution (New York, Cambridge*; Cambridge University Press, 1959).

'Science, Politics and the Novelist; Or, the Fish and the Net', *Kenyon Review*, 23 (1961) 1–17.

Science and Government (Cambridge, Mass: Harvard University Press, 1961.* London: Oxford University Press, 1961. Toronto: S. J. Reginald Saunders, 1961. New York: New American Library, 1962).

Variety of Men (London: Macmillan, 1967. New York: Scribner, 1967*).

Public Affairs (London: Macmillan, 1971. New York: Scribner, 1971*).

Trollope: His Life and Art (London: Macmillan, 1975. New York: Scribner, 1975*).

SECONDARY REFERENCES

Adams, R. W., 'Pomp and Circumstance: C. P. Snow', *Atlantic Monthly*, 214 (1964) 95.

Allen, Walter, *The Novel Today* (London: British Council, 1960).

—— *Reading a Novel* (London: Phoenix House, 1956).

—— *The Modern Novel in Britain and the United States* (New York: Dutton, 1964).

Bailliett, W., 'Biographical Note', *Saturday Review*, 38, II (8 Jan, 1955) 9.

Benedikz, B. S. (ed.), *On the Novel: A Present to Walter Allen on his 60th Birthday from his Friends and Colleagues* (London: Dent, 1971). Includes Snow's 'Trollope; The Psychological Stream'.

Bergonzi, Bernard, The Situation of the Novel (London: Pelican, 1972).

—— 'The World of Lewis Eliot', Twentieth Century, 167 (1960) 214.

Bradbury, Malcolm, 'The Novel', in The Twentieth Century Mind, ed. C. B. Cox and A. E. Dyson (Oxford: OUP Paperbacks, 1974).

—— Possibilities: Essays on the State of the Novel (Oxford: OUP Paperbacks, 1974).

Brady, Charles A., 'The British Novel Today', Thought, 34 (winter 1959–60) 518.

Bragg, Melvyn, interview with Kingsley Amis, Listener, 20 Feb 1975, p. 240.

Bremner, Marjorie, review of C. P. Snow's The Affair, Twentieth Century, 168 (1960) 89.

Brophy, Brigid, 'The Novel as Take-Over Bid', Listener, 3 Oct 1963, p. 501.

Burgess, Anthony, 'The Corruption of the Exotic', Listener, 26 Sept 1963, p. 465.

—— 'Powers that Be', Encounter, 24 (1965) 71.

'Chubb Fellow', New Yorker, 37, no. 44 (16 Dec, 1961) 44.

Cooper, William, C. P. Snow (London: British Council, 1959).

Daiches, David, The Novel and the Modern World (Chicago: University of Chicago Press, 1960).

Davis, R. G., C. P. Snow (New York: Columbia University Press, 1965).

Dennis, N., 'Under the Combination Room', Encounter, 17 (1961) 51.

Finkelstein, S., 'The Art and Science of C. P. Snow', Mainstream, 14 (1961) 31.

Fison, Peter, 'A Reply to Bernard Bergonzi's "World of Lewis Eliot"', Twentieth Century, 167 (1960) 568.

Flint, R. W., 'The Undying Apocalypse' (review of C. P. Snow's Homecomings), Partisan Review, 24 (winter 1957) 139.

Fraser, G. S., The Modern Writer and his World (London: Deutsch, 1964).

Fuller, Edmund, 'Snow: Spokesman of Two Communities', Books with Men Behind Them (New York: Random House, 1962).

Fyvel, T. R., 'Problems of the Modern Novelist', Listener, 21 Apr 1955, p. 708.

Gardner, A., 'A Literary Owl Who Doesn't Give a Hoot', Saturday Review, 4 Mar 1961, p. 53.

Gardner, Helen, 'The World of C. P. Snow', New Statesman, 55 (1958) 409.

Grandsen, K. W., 'Thoughts on Contemporary Fiction', Review of English Literature, 1 (1960) 7.

Greacen, Robert, 'Profile of C. P. Snow', Humanist, 73 (1958) 9.

—— 'The World of C. P. Snow', Texas Quarterly, 4 (1961 Part 2) 266.

—— The World of C. P. Snow, with a bibliography by B. Stone (London: Scorpion Press, 1962).

Green, Martin, 'A Literary Defence of the Two Cultures', Kenyon Review, 24 (1962) 731.

—— 'Lionel Trilling and the Two Cultures', Essays in Criticism, 13 (1963) 375.

Halio, J. L., 'Snow's Literary Limitations', Northwest Review, 5 (winter 1962) 97.

Hall, W., 'The Humanism of Snow', Wisconsin Studies in Contemporary Literature, 4 (1963) 199.

Hamilton, K., 'C. P. Snow and Political Man', Queen's Quarterly, 69 (1962) 416.

Hartley, L. P., 'The Novelist and his Material', The Times Literary Supplement, 15 Aug 1958, p. iv.

Heppenstall, Rayner, The Fourfold Tradition (London: Barrie, 1961).

Hilton, Frank, 'Britain's New Class', Encounter, 10 (1958) 59.

Hoggart, R., 'The Unsuspected Audience', New Statesman, 56 (1958) 308.

Huxley, Aldous, Literature and Science (London: Chatto & Windus, 1963).

Johnson, Pamela Hansford, Important to Me (New York: Scribner, 1974).

—— 'Modern Fiction and the English Understatement', *The Times Literary Supplement*, 7 Aug 1959, p. 111.

—— 'The Debate about the Novel', *New Statesman*, 9 Aug 1958, p. 172.

—— 'Three Novelists and the Drawing of Character: C. P. Snow, Joyce Cary and Ivy Compton-Burnett', in *Essays and Studies* (London, 1950) p. 82.

—— 'With Prejudice', *Windmill*, 1 (1944) 1.

Karl, Frederick R., *The Politics of Conscience: the Novels of C. P. Snow* (Carbondale: Southern Illinois University Press, 1963).

—— *A Reader's Guide to the Contemporary English Novel* (New York: Farrar, Straus & Giroux, 1972).

Kazin, Alfred, 'A Brilliant Boy from the Midlands', in *Contemporaries* (Boston: Little, Brown, 1962) p. 171.

Kermode, Frank, 'Beckett, Snow and Pure Poverty', *Encounter*, 15 (1960) 73.

—— 'Myth, Reality and Fiction', *Listener*, 30 Aug 1962, p. 311.

—— 'The House of Fiction: Interviews with Seven English Novelists', *Partisan Review*, 30 (spring 1963) 74.

Ketels, V. B., 'Shaw, Snow and the new man', *Personalist*, 47 (1966) 520.

Kostelanetz, R. (ed.), *On Contemporary Literature* (New York: Avon Books, 1969).

Kunitz, S. J. and Howard Haycraft, 'C. P. Snow', *Twentieth Century Authors: First Supplement* (New York: Wilson, 1955).

Latham, Earl, 'The Managerialization of the Campus', *Public Administration Review*, 19 (1959) 48.

Larkin, Philip, 'The Writer in his Age', *London Magazine*, 4 (1957) 46.

Leavis, F. R., 'The Significance of C. P. Snow', *Spectator*, 9 Mar 1962, p. 297.

Lehan, Richard, 'The Divided World: *The Masters* Examined' in *Six Contemporary Novels*, ed. W. O. S. Sutherland (Austin: University of Texas Press, 1962).

'The Many-Sided Life of Sir Charles Snow', *Life*, 7 Apr 1961, p. 134.

Lindegren, Carl C., 'He is no Scientist but an Administrator', *Humanist*, 84 (1964) 91.

Lloyd, Quentin, 'My Relationship with C. P. Snow: Ronald Miller Interviewed by Q. Lloyd', *Time and Tide*, 13 Sept 1962, p. 16.

Lodge, David, 'The Contemporary Novel and all that Jazz', *London Magazine*, 2 (1962) 73.

Lovell, A. C. B., *et al.*, 'The Two Cultures: A Discussion of C. P. Snow's Views', *Encounter*, 13 (1959) 67.

Macdonald, A., 'Imagery in Snow', *University Review*, 33 (1966) 32.

Mandel, E. W., 'C. P. Snow's Fantasy of Politics', *Queen's Quarterly*, 69 (1962) 24.

Manning, Olivia, 'Notes on the Future of the Novel', *The Times Literary Supplement*, 15 Aug 1958, p. vi.

Marcus, Steven, 'Intellectuals, Scientists and the Future', *Commentary*, 29 (1960) 165.

Martin, Graham, 'Novelists of Three Decades: Evelyn Waugh, Graham Greene, C. P. Snow', in *The Modern Age: Pelican Guide to English Literature* (London: Pelican, 1961).

Mayne, Richard, 'The Club Armchair', *Encounter*, 21 (1963) 76.

Millgate, Michael, 'Structure and Style in the novels of C. P. Snow', *Review of English Literature*, 1 (1960) 34.

Miner, Earl, 'C. P. Snow and the Realistic Novel', *Nation*, 190 (1960) 554.

Moskin, J. R., 'Conversations with C. P. Snow', *Saturday Review World*, 6 Apr 1974, p. 20.

Murray, B. O., 'Snow: Grounds for Re-appraisal', *Personalist*, 47 (1966) 91.

Newby, P. H., *The Novel: 1945–1950* (London: British Council, 1951).

Nott, Kathleen, 'The Type to Which the Whole Creation Moves? Thoughts on the Snow Saga', *Encounter*, 18 (1962) 87.

—— 'Whose Culture?', *Listener*, 12 Apr 1962, p. 631, and 19 Apr 1962, p. 677.

Phelps, Gilbert, 'The Novel Today', in *The Modern Age: Pelican Guide to English Literature* (London: Pelican, 1961).

Proctor, Mortimer, *The English University Novel* (Berkeley: University of California Press, 1957).

Pryce-Jones, Alan, 'The Making of an Idea', *The Times Literary Supplement*, 15 Aug 1958.

Putt, S. Gorley, 'Technique and Culture: Three Cambridge Portraits', *Essays and Studies*, 14 (London, 1961) 17.

Rabinovitz, R., *The Reaction Against Experiment in the English Novel: 1950–1960* (New York: Columbia University Press, 1967).

Raleigh, John H., 'Victorian Morals and the Modern Novel', *Partisan Review*, 25 (1958) 241.

Read, Herbert, 'Mood of the Month-10: Comment on Snow's Rede Lecture', *London Magazine*, 6 (1959) 39.

Interview with C. P. Snow', *Review of English Literature*, 3 (1962) 91.

Robbe-Grille, Alain, 'The Case for the New Novel', *New Statesman*, 17 Feb 1961, p. 261.

Saal, R. W., 'Sir Charles Snow', *Saturday Review*, 43 (1960) 15.

Shapiro, Charles *Contemporary British Novelists* (Carbondale: Southern Illinois University Press, 1965).

Sokolov, R. A., 'Strangers and Brothers', *Newsweek*, 17 Aug 1970, p. 88.

Spender, Stephen, *The Struggle of the Modern* (Berkeley: University of California Press, 1963).

Stanford, Derek, 'C. P. Snow: Novelist as Fox', *Meanjin*, 19 (1960) 236.

—— 'Thoughts on Contemporary Literature', *Contemporary Review*, 191 (1957), 234.

—— 'Report from London', *Western Review*, 21 (Summer 1957), 293.

—— 'A Disputed Master: Snow and his Critics', *Month*, 29 (1963) 91.

Stanford, Raney, 'Personal Politics in the Novels of C. P. Snow', *Critique*, 11 (1958) 16.

—— 'The Achievement of C. P. Snow', *Western Humanities Review*, 16 (1962) 43.

Story, Jack Trevor, 'Lid off the Lords' (review of C. P. Snow's *In Their Wisdom*), *Listener*, 10 Oct 1974, p. 482.

Swinden, Patrick, 'The World of C. P. Snow', *Critical Quarterly*, 15 (winter 1973) 297.

Thale, Jerome, 'C. P. Snow: The Art of Worldiness', *Kenyon Review*, 22 (1960) 621.

—— *C. P. Snow* (New York: Scribner, 1964).

'Experience of a Lifetime,' *The Times Literary Supplement*, 20 June 1958, p. 345.

'Experiment in Prose', *Times Literary Supplement*, 17 Aug 1956, p. ii.

'A Matter of money' (review of C. P. Snow's *In Their Wisdom*), *The Times Literary Supplement*, 11 Oct 1974, p. 1109.

'A Question of Brains', *The Times Literary Supplement*, 23 Mar 1962, p. 201.

'The Novelist's World', *The Times Literary Supplement*, 6 Sep 1957, p. 553.

'Two Views of Fiction', *The Times Literary Supplement*, 7 Nov 1958, p. 641.

'Uncommitted Talents', *The Times Literary Supplement*, 29 Aug 1952, p. iii.

'The World of Power and Groups' (review of C. P. Snow's *Last Things*), *The Times Literary Supplement*, 23 Oct 1970, p. 1223.

Trilling, Lionel, 'The Novel Alive or Dead', in *A Gathering of Fugitives* (Boston: Beacon Press, 1956).

—— 'Science, Literature and Culture', *Commentary*, 33 (1962) 461.

—— 'Manners, Morals and the Novel', *The Liberal Imagination* (New York: Viking Press, 1950).

Vogel, A. W., 'The Academic World of Snow', *Twentieth Century Literature*, 9 (1963) 143.

Wagner, Geoffrey, 'Sociology and Fiction', *Twentieth Century*, 167 (1960) 108.

Wain, John, 'The Conflict of Forms in Contemporary English Literature', *Critical Quarterly*, 4 (summer 1962) 101.

Wall, Stephen, 'Reputations 10: the novels of C. P. Snow', *London Magazine*, new series 4 (1964) 68.

Watson, K., 'Snow and the New Men', *English*, 15 (1965) 134.

Weintraub, Stanley (ed.), *C. P. Snow: a Spectrum—Science, Criticism, Fiction* (New York: Scribner, 1963).

West, Paul, *The Modern Novel* (London: Hutchinson, 1963).

Williams, Raymond, 'Realism and the Contemporary Novel', *Partisan Review*, 26 (spring 1959) 200.

Wilson, Angus, 'Diversity and Depth', *The Times Literary Supplement*, 15 Aug 1958.

Wilson, Edmund, 'An Interview with Edmund Wilson', *New Yorker*, 2 June 1962, p. 118.

—— 'The Workaday World the Novelist Never Enters', *The Times Literary Supplement*, 9 Sep 1960, p. vii.

Index

The names of characters from fiction and drama are marked with an asterisk.